WISH YOU DEAD

Rebecca Westcott

■Scholastic

Published in the UK by Scholastic, 2025
Scholastic, Bosworth Avenue, Warwick, CV34 6UQ
Scholastic Ireland, 89E Lagan Road, Dublin Industrial Estate,
Glasnevin, Dublin, D11 HP5F

SCHOLASTIC and associated logos are trademarks and/or
registered trademarks of Scholastic Inc.

Text © Rebecca Westcott, 2025
Cover illustration by Erick Dávila © Scholastic, 2025

The moral rights of the author have been asserted by them.

ISBN 978 0702 31847 4

A CIP catalogue record for this book
is available from the British Library.

All rights reserved.
This book is sold subject to the condition that it shall not,
by way of trade or otherwise, be lent, hired out or otherwise circulated in
any form of binding or cover other than that in which it is published. No
part of this publication may be reproduced, stored in a retrieval system,
or transmitted in any form or by any other means (electronic, mechanical,
photocopying, recording or otherwise) without prior
written permission of Scholastic Limited.

Printed in the UK
Paper made from wood grown in sustainable forests
and other controlled sources.

1 3 5 7 9 10 8 6 4 2

This is a work of fiction. Any resemblance to actual people,
events or locales is entirely coincidental.

www.scholastic.co.uk

For safety or quality concerns:
UK: www.scholastic.co.uk/productinformation
EU: www.scholastic.ie/productinformation

For everyone who knows that, deep down, they are a little bit magic. And definitely for all the witches…

PROLOGUE

Morgana Merrick was twelve years old when she killed a woman. To the outside observer, it might have appeared that there was no consequence, no recompense. There was no arrest or trial. No having to answer for what she had done or face the judgement of others.

It would be a mistake to think that she got away with it, though.

Karma is like that.

It's a real witch.

CHAPTER 1

Once could be excused as a mistake. Anyone can mess up once; Morgana accepts that. But twice? Hell, no. Twice isn't a mistake. Twice is a decision. Twice is a choice. Twice is asking for trouble.

She throws her phone on the bed. Outside, a car horn blasts through the early-morning silence and she knows that if she doesn't hurry up, Art will leave without her. And there is absolutely no way that she's prepared to walk to school today. Not in this heat. Not when she's got a problem to take care of. She's let this slide long enough – Ro needs dealing with, and fast.

Slicking on some lipgloss, she gives herself an admiring glance in the mirror. A hint of blush on her cheeks to add some contour and ensure that her face doesn't look too pale. Dramatic eyeliner and sweeping dark lashes that have become her trademark look. Her hair hangs just below her chin, the dark black offering a striking contrast to the two white stripes that fall on either side of her face. Morgana knows a couple of facts about her "Mallen streak" – the first is that it comes from the Latin word *malignus*, which means wicked or damned, doomed from birth. The second is that it is hereditary. In fact, the streak is one of only three things that her mother left her, which she feels is pleasingly fitting.

The horn sounds again, more urgent this time, and, with a last glance to check that her make-up is perfect, Morgana grabs her phone and bag and leaves the room, ignoring the wet towels lying on the bedroom floor and the crumpled mess of her bed sheets. Mabel or Mavis, or whatever her name is, will sort all that when she finishes cleaning the kitchen, which, as Morgana had a desire for pancakes this morning, might take her a hot minute.

She makes her way downstairs, letting her hand glide along the thick oak banister that sweeps round the wide curve of the impressive staircase. The entrance foyer is bathed in sunlight, streaming in though the floor-to-ceiling wall of glass that their father repeatedly tells her and Art is one of the main features of Pendragon Hall, along with the heated pool inside the room that he refers to as the *orangery* and which Morgana insistently calls the conservatory just to piss him off. The house is incredible, she knows that really – but it's only that. A house. Not a home. Pendragon Hall has all the soul of a hotel and Morgana treats it with the same level of disdain, slamming the heavy front door behind her now with unnecessary force and registering the crashing sound of something falling off the wall with vague satisfaction. With any luck it will be yet another photograph of Art – she's up to three now. Her father will threaten to take the cost of repairing the frame out of her generous allowance, but he won't do it. Not when money is the only thing he actually does give her.

"OK, OK, I'm coming," she mutters, opening the passenger door and folding herself inside, while simultaneously lowering her sunglasses on to her face. It's bright, despite the early hour. "What's the big rush?"

In the driver's seat, Art starts the car. He attempts to, anyway. The Jaguar has seen better days and even though their father has told him repeatedly that it belongs on the scrapheap and that he'll replace it, Art is weirdly attached to the old thing that once belonged to his mother. The engine turns over in protest at being asked to wake up and Morgana is about to join in with a complaint of her own when it judders into life.

Art pumps a jubilant fist in the air and mutters a quiet, "*Well done, Iggy,*" before heading down the perfectly gravelled drive and between the ornate stone pillars that stand sentry on either side of the entrance gate. The raven, who Morgana has spotted sitting in the tree outside her window for the last two days, is perched on top of one of the pillars, staring beadily at them as they pass through. She shivers, despite the warmth in the air, remembering the stories she's been told about the birds who are said to be the foretellers of doom.

It's a ten-minute drive, but Morgana only needs two to deal with her problem. Opening her phone, she looks again at the offending message that Ro posted online late last night during what was quite clearly a sleepover at her house. It's a photo of their group, *her* group, posing for the camera while trying to act natural, as if they've been caught unawares and always look this good, which is farcical when everyone knows that they'll have rejected at least sixteen versions of the same photo before agreeing on this one. There should be five girls in the picture, but someone is missing and Morgana has had just about as much as she can take of Ro's pathetic power games.

"Can you believe this?" She waves her phone in front of Art and he flicks his eyes towards it before batting her hand away.

"What is it? And don't distract me when I'm driving with something that's non-urgent."

Morgana supresses a sigh. It's a whole year until she can get her driving licence and the thought of having to be chauffeured everywhere by Art is infuriating. She doesn't understand why everyone is obsessed with her brother. She can grudgingly admit that he's not a troll to look at (although most people don't have the misfortune of seeing him when he's just woken up, before he's styled his hair into its blond surfer flop) but his chilled-out, sloth-like approach to everything in his life is at extreme odds with her love of action.

She also can't wait until she can arrive at school in something other than a clapped-out old Jaguar. Their father has promised her any car of her choosing *within reason* for her seventeenth birthday and she's already eyeing up a sweet hot-pink Mercedes G wagon that she intends to convince him has the best safety ratings for his little princess.

He'll buy it; she knows he will. Gordon Merrick's love language is throwing obscene amounts of money at his offspring, in the hope that they'll leave him in peace to focus on what really matters in life – building his business empire and making more money. Besides, as the big man in Avalon, he has connections everywhere and there's no way he'll have to pay the full price. Everyone is always desperate to curry favour with the man who can make gold out of stone.

"It *is* urgent, actually." She stares at the screen, narrowing her eyes before zooming in closer on the photograph. "Ro has posted yet another picture with hashtag *sistersforlife*. Without *me*. She invited the others over last night and then posted about it. I mean, it's got to be deliberate at this point. I've noticed it for a while, her trying to weasel her way into everyone's good books – and now this."

They're all there, pouting out at her in high definition.

Iris, the tiny typical English Rose with blue eyes and long blonde hair, looking like butter wouldn't melt, gazing adoringly at the girl beside her.

Maz, poker-straight long brown hair, expertly applied lipstick, gorgeous high cheekbones that she got from her Chinese mother and matching pearl earrings and necklace that she got from her American father and which would look ridiculous on anyone else, smiling just a bit too hard.

Lettie, posing as if she's on the photo-shoot of her dreams, her long black box braids cascading like a waterfall around her face and her perfect smile highlighting the bronze glow of her cheeks against her dark skin.

And Ro, honey-blonde afro hair piled up in a high messy bun. Foolish, reckless Ro, standing in the middle of the group and staring into the camera lens. Right into Morgana's eyes, taunting her, challenging her.

"How dare she?" she mutters.

"Yeah, sounds terrible," drawls Art, finally shifting into fourth gear. "Imagine posting a picture of your friends online. Although that 'sisters' hashtag is a bit cringe."

The "Sisters" name *is* lame; Morgana should never have let them choose it. She flicks her hair out of her face and shoots Art a glare. "I don't think you quite understand. This is a power move. Ro invited the rest of the girls over without me and she wants me to know. Along with the rest of the world."

Art shrugs and indicates to turn right. "So what?"

Morgana scowls at him. "So, *I* get to decide who's invited and who's not, and I'm not about to be overthrown by *her*." She turns her attention back to her phone and starts to tap at the screen. "But no worries – she's an inconvenience, that's all."

"Overthrown?" He shakes his head. "You're not the queen of Avalon, Morgana."

Morgana rolls her eyes and pulls down the sun visor to check her lipgloss. Such an ignorant statement does not deserve a response.

"What's the plan then?" Art pulls the car to a halt at the crossing, waiting for the wave of lower-school kids to meander across the road, clearly in no rush to get to school.

Morgana slams the sun visor shut, finishes typing and presses *send*, before flashing him a grin.

"I don't plan," she tells him. "I act. And if Ro is still one of the *Sisters* by the end of today, I will be extremely surprised."

Art drums his fingers on Iggy's steering wheel, finally looking across at her.

"You do know that getting what you want by attacking someone else isn't good vibes, don't you?"

Morgana snorts. "As if you care. And you can spare me your motivational surf quotes, Art. I'm not one of the pick-me girls who think you're Avalon's answer to the Dalai Lama."

"Whatever." Art swings the car into a student parking space and kills the engine. "I'm heading to the beach after school so you'll have to walk home. We can order takeaway when I'm back – unless you want to eat whatever godawful casserole Mabel has left for us?"

Morgana shudders and opens the door. "As if." Their father left on a business trip a few days ago and the next few weeks of the housekeeper's casserole looms before them like a culinary wasteland.

She swings her long legs out of the car, enjoying the stretch in her calf muscles as her toes make contact with the ground. She needs to find the others and take a temperature check of how her revelatory text message has been received. She's as gutted as the rest of them, she really is, and she feels so, so bad about telling them what Ro has been doing behind their backs. She wouldn't have said a word – she prizes loyalty above all else, *obviously* – but the sight of Ro getting up close and personal with Jayce when they all know that Lettie is desperately in love with him was too much. It's all *so* messy and awful and she feels super stressed about it.

"Morgana?" Art leans across the front seat to get her attention. "Just remember what Dad always says. If you ask for what you want—"

"Then you'd better be prepared to get it," finishes Morgana. A brief, rare smile passes between them and then it's gone. She rearranges her face to convey tragic, conflicted, worried friend and then walks towards the Year Eleven entrance. She's got this. Nobody shapeshifts better than Morgana Merrick and only a fool would think twice about going up against her.

Today, that fool is Ro. Tomorrow it will be someone else. It's not pleasant, throwing your friend under the bus, but Morgana has no choice. If that's the price for being the most popular, loved, feared, admired girl at Avalon Academy, then she's willing to make them pay.

Whatever the cost.

CHAPTER 2

"I just can't believe that Ro could be so two-faced," snipes Lettie, for what feels like the millionth time in the last two days. "I *told* her that I was totally into Jayce, so what the hell was she doing, going after him like that?"

Iris nods in sympathy, reaching for her drink and taking a loud slurp. "I'm so sorry, Lettie. I can't imagine what Ro was thinking."

"*Je suis très triste.*" Lettie dabs at her eyes. "That means *I am so sad.*"

Morgana rolls her eyes. Ever since Lettie found out that her great-great-great-grandfather was French, she's been even more unbearable than usual. Leaning back in her plastic chair, she lets her attention turn to the other occupants of the Surf Shack. There's a queue of people lining up at the counter inside but the majority are out here on the wooden decking that juts out of the Shack and on to the beach. This place is dead for most of the year, but now it's finally summer things are starting to heat up and there's quite a crowd. It's mostly kids from Avalon Academy who flock down to the beach after school. They choose to avoid the dodgy school canteen and instead save their lunch money to spend on burgers, hot dogs and milkshakes at the Shack. Its prime position, right on the sand, makes it the ideal spot to watch the surfers and catch up on the latest dramas. Morgana isn't interested in the surfers but she makes it her business to always know what is going on, who's into who and where she might need to focus her energies.

"It's not as if Jayce is even all that, right, Morgana?" adds Maz, pulling her back into the conversation. "If Ro was going to betray a Sister, then at least choose someone half decent. I heard that his dad works for an estate agent, but not as the owner or anything. Only a complete loser would try to get it on with a reject like him."

"Maz." Iris's voice holds a hint of admonishment. "Think about what you're saying. Lettie had serious feelings for Jayce."

"Yeah, Maz." Morgana yawns delicately. "Are you calling *Lettie* a loser?"

Maz slaps her hand to her mouth in fake horror and turns to look at Lettie. "God, I wasn't thinking. I'm *so* sorry."

"It's OK." Lettie sniffs, as oblivious as always. "I know you didn't mean me. But why would Ro hurt me? What have I ever done to her?"

"You've not done anything," says Maz, bored now. "Anyway, what do you think of my new sunglasses? They were insanely expensive but you know what my mum is like. I tried telling her that I was OK with the pair that cost half the amount but she reckons that anything costing less than five hundred quid is a false investment…"

Morgana zones out of what is no doubt about to be a lengthy monologue from Maz about how much money has been spent on her this week by her wealthy parents. She may be in an equally privileged position with no financial worries, but she hasn't forgotten her life before Avalon. The canvas holdall, the second thing that her mother left her with, is still hidden at the back of her walk-in wardrobe, with an emergency stash of notes tucked into the inside pocket just in case.

She sits for a few minutes, enjoying the feel of the sun on her face and the crashing sound of the waves, letting it wash over her as she observes the scene from behind her own expensive sunglasses. It's the closest she's got to relaxing all day, but the moment is short-lived. The crowd parts, as if royalty is approaching, and Morgana watches as Art and his entourage stroll into view, surfboards at the ready as they head down the steps at the side of the Shack. Ginny, his girlfriend, is tucked under Art's free arm and Lance, his best friend, strides alongside. Vivi, who lives next door to Pendragon Hall, scuttles nervously behind, and Morgana feels a familiar pulse of irritation. The girl follows Ginny like a small, devoted puppy. The difference between the two girls couldn't be starker – Vivi's washed-out face, unbrushed hair and boring clothes seem even more mundane beside Ginny's statuesque figure and long white mermaid hair. Even tucked beneath a beanie, it is mesmerising. It's hard to see why they are friends, but Morgana has come to the conclusion that Ginny likes the attention.

"Waves are cooking today, Art!" yells a boy from Morgana's maths class.

Art nods in response but doesn't look over and Morgana rolls her eyes. He's always *in the zone* before he surfs. She's not entirely convinced that *the zone* is a real thing but she grudgingly admits it adds to his mystique.

"Are you going to give us something to look at, Lance?" calls Maz, her voice oozing with suggestion.

Morgana resists the urge to slap her for pulling his focus in their direction but it's too late and Lance is walking across to them with that arrogant swagger that screams *attention-seeker* to anyone in a two-mile vicinity.

"Hey, gorgeous, are you here to watch me?" Lance ignores Maz, instead standing too close to Morgana, his surfboard tucked under one arm and his wetsuit bunched up round his waist, revealing his perfectly flexed abs. His distinctive sandalwood and vanilla cologne, which Morgana knows for a fact costs more than the average person spends on a week's worth of grocery shopping, wafts on the warm breeze. Beside her, Morgana senses Maz inhaling deeply, as if she's trying to absorb Lance into her lungs.

Morgana shudders and slowly lowers her sunglasses, letting them dangle from the fingers of one hand. Lance might have been Art's best friend since for ever and he might spend more time in their house than her own father, but he makes her skin crawl. It was OK last year, but ever since she turned sixteen a few months ago, he's been looking at her with something in his eyes that reminds her of a hungry wolf.

And right now, Morgana feels like Little Red Riding Hood.

But not at the beginning, scared and vulnerable. No, she's Little Red at the end of the story, ready to finish this.

"It rather depends on what you're going to be showing us," she purrs, because sometimes it's good to give wolves enough rope to hang themselves.

Lance flexes his muscles and raises an eyebrow at her, leaning in close enough for her to smell the sunscreen on his skin. "So, d'you like what you see so far?"

Morgana purses her lips and tilts her head, as if in thought. The people closest to them have gone quiet, soaking up this interaction between the most popular girl in Year Eleven and the most daring, risk-taking boy in Year Twelve.

"I've been wondering when you'd see what's right in front of you," breathes Lance, putting his mouth next to her ear so that nobody else can hear. "Just say the word, M."

Morgana reaches out one perfectly manicured hand and forces herself to place it on his bare chest, pushing him away.

"Get back to me when you can surf a wave without bailing," she tells him, her voice loud and her message clear. "Now off you pop and try not to wipe out – it's just embarrassing when you can't even stay upright on your board."

Lance straightens. He grins at her, although Morgana sees a pleasing flash of annoyance in his eyes.

"What's *embarrassing* is your obsession with me," he says, sweeping his shoulder-length hair away from his face. "I'll catch you later."

Then he leaps off the decking and on to the sand, chasing after Art, Ginny and Vivi who have continued down the steps and on to the beach, and who are now almost at the water's edge. Morgana watches as they all hand their phones to Vivi, who settles herself down on the sand with their possessions like the good little surfer groupie that she is, before running into the water as if they're auditioning for an episode of *Baywatch*.

"Phew, there was some extreme heat coming off you two," says Lettie, fanning herself with her hand.

Morgana turns back to her, unable to repress a scowl. "What are you on about?"

Maz laughs, although it sounds forced. "Come off it, Morgana. The chemistry between you and Lance is full-on – it's definitely going to end up in something hot. I didn't know where to look!"

Morgana shakes her head. "The only chemistry between me and that idiot is like hydrogen and oxygen and the only thing it's going to result in is a freaking explosion. And not the good kind."

"I had that kind of chemistry with Jayce," whines Lettie. "Until Ro ruined it. And I thought she was *mon amie*."

"Lettie, you've never spoken a single word to Jayce," snaps Morgana, and then, when they all stare at her wide-eyed, she reaches out her hand and pats Lettie's arm, quickly resuming the role of magnanimous benefactor. "What I mean is, you might not have been that compatible, after all. And if he couldn't even be bothered to find the time to talk to you, then he's not worth it."

"He's *so* not worth it," says Iris, quickly backing Morgana up. Iris, the delicate little flower of the group, just can't handle a second of conflict or upset.

Lettie gulps and then nods.

"You're right," she tells them. "Thanks, Morgana. At least I know you've got my back, even if that cow Ro hasn't. That's why we're Sisters."

"Of course." Morgana bestows her most beatific smile on Lettie, swallowing down the urge to throw up. "And Sisters stick together – *true* Sisters, anyway."

"So what now?" asks Maz, playing with the necklace round her neck. "What are we going to do about Ro? We can't let her get away with being disloyal."

Morgana rests her chin on her hands and looks thoughtful. This is the stage of the operation when she says nothing. She's planted the seed – it's up to the rest of them to bring home the harvest.

"You're right," says Lettie. "Otherwise it's like we're saying that anyone can betray one of us and there won't be any consequences."

Maz nods. "That's a good point, actually. It's not just about Ro, is it?"

Morgana nods slowly.

"Are you saying … she's out?" whispers Iris. "Out of the Sisters?"

"It's the only way," says Maz sadly.

"So we're all in agreement?" Lettie glances round the table. "Ro is out, yeah? She's gone?"

"We haven't really got any other choice, have we?" Iris's voice is filled with worry. "It's not even like it's up to us — she did it to herself."

"Absolutely," says Maz. "You get what you give. That's how it works."

Everyone mutters their agreement. Out on the water, Lance and Art start paddling rapidly ahead of a wave and the focus of everyone in the Shack is on them and their surfboards. Morgana puts her sunglasses back on and leans back in her seat, inscrutable behind the dark lenses — which is just the way she likes it. The girls in front of her sit up straighter, each one of them thirsty for attention from either Art or Lance, the gods of surf. Morgana watches, but she isn't really looking. Instead, she's preparing herself for what is undoubtedly coming. Ro was absent from school today but she won't be able to stay away from them for long, Morgana is certain of that.

In fact, any second now...

"Hey." The voice is quiet, hesitant, and it warms Morgana's heart to hear the way it trembles. She doesn't turn her head because that's not what she does. If Ro wants her attention, then it's on her to enter Morgana's line of sight. "Can we talk?"

It's a plea and if there's something else that Morgana doesn't do, it's neediness. She glances down at the beach, where Vivi is now on her feet and videoing the boys on her phone, no doubt tasked with filming every moment in the hope of capturing some Insta-worthy footage. It's pathetic how desperate she is for their approval. She'd be far more respected by everyone if she told them all to hold their own damn bags and went off to do her own thing, but Morgana knows there's no chance of Vivi doing that. She's too *nice*.

From Morgana, that's not a compliment.

"Morgana?" The voice is slightly louder now, and the other girls turn to look at Ro, who is shuffling from one foot to the other, appearing increasingly uncomfortable. The kids nearby pick up on the tension and silence spreads across the decking once more, as everyone tunes in to this new drama. Morgana resists the urge to stand up and tell them all that they're welcome.

"Did you hear something?" Maz asks Lettie snippily, looking from left to right. "I could have sworn I heard something."

"Nope." Lettie shakes her head. "Didn't hear a thing."

"Me neither," says Iris, although her voice is more hesitant that the others. If anyone is likely to cave, it's sweet, people-pleasing Iris.

Morgana sometimes wonders just how far Iris would let herself be pushed before she actually said no. It's a fun way to spend an idle few minutes, dreaming up scenarios that might make Iris defend herself.

"Morgana, please?" repeats Ro. "I want to sort this out."

Morgana inspects her nails, checking for chips. Maybe she'll add in a pedicure and a massage to her regular manicure appointment at Avalon's only beauty salon. Her neck muscles have been feeling tense lately – probably because of all this ridiculousness.

She rolls her head from side to side, stretching out the tendons. This is getting boring now. Raising a perfectly shaped eyebrow at Ro, she acknowledges her existence for one last time, and then she lets her gaze drift out to sea. The message is clear. Ro is over. She might still be breathing but she's a ghost, and the best she can hope for now is to be ignored.

Because this is Morgana's power. She can raise people to the highest heights or she can slam them lower than they can imagine, and all without a single word. Ro is dead and Morgana didn't have to lift a finger. She doesn't even look as Ro slinks away, her shoulders slumped and her eyes on the sandy wooden planks below her feet. She doesn't need to. Everyone else is watching and they all know what just happened. Which means that none of them will be as foolish as to try the same thing themselves.

Morgana watches as Lance wipes out on a wave and allows herself a small smile. All around, people start to talk again but she can still hear the silence that she is capable of summoning with a flick of her hair. That silence is what feeds her – the tense stillness that signifies her strength.

"Well, that was awkward," says Lettie, exhaling loudly. "Thanks for dealing with her, Morgana."

Morgana turns, her eyes wide with her best *shocked* expression plastered on her face. "I didn't do anything," she tells her. "It was all of you who decided to kick her out. Everyone was watching too. I support your choices, of course I do – but I am worried about how Ro is going to cope with such a public rejection."

Iris pales and beside her Maz scowls and opens her mouth as if she's about to object. Morgana's gaze swings on to her, the glint in her eyes reminding Maz of who she is and what she is capable of, and the other girl's lips clamp firmly shut.

"Maybe we were too harsh," murmurs Lettie. "Perhaps we should have heard her out."

"Perhaps," agrees Morgana, leaning down to pick up her bag. "But it's done now. I just hope she isn't too hurt." She nods at the girls, her face a perfect mixture of supportive and concerned and then she walks away, before she ruins it all by laughing.

Because it's a lie.

Hurting Ro, while reminding everyone who is in control here, was the entire point.

CHAPTER 3

The house is empty. Morgana drops her bag by the front door and walks into the kitchen, opening the huge American fridge and choosing a bottle of juice before heading back to the entrance foyer, her eyes drawn as always to the photos on the wall. The frame that fell off with this morning's enthusiastic door slam is lying on the dresser, presumably placed there by Mabel/Mavis when she came in to do the housekeeping earlier. Morgana is pleased to see that, once again, it's a photograph of Art – this time one of him aged ten, receiving a lifeguarding certificate. Which make it five out of five and counting.

Not that this is surprising – the odds are in her favour when pictures of Art outnumber those of Morgana by four to one. Over the last few years Gordon has attempted to add some pictures of his only daughter to the wall of fame, but he'd have to photograph her daily to make up for the lifetime he missed. Not that it's entirely their father's fault – ever since she moved to Avalon four years ago, Morgana has felt distinctly uncomfortable letting anyone take her photograph. She's aware that it doesn't make sense but the idea of someone capturing her image makes her feel uneasy, as if they might see more of her than just what's on the outside. Almost every picture taken of her is a selfie.

Wandering into the orangery, Morgana checks on the plants that Mabel/Mavis is instructed to water every day. No expense has been spared on filling the room with exotic species that thrive in the warm, humid air. She runs her hand gently over the larger leaves and breathes in deeply, enjoying the feeling of being alone. The last few days – with Ro's pathetic attempts at trying to exclude her – have dragged up some uncomfortable memories of a time when she wasn't in control the way she is now, a time when she felt like the victim.

Throwing herself on to the chaise longue that their father had shipped over from Italy – there's a total ban on anyone eating or drinking within a two-metre radius of its exquisite velvet cover – she lets her mind roam over the recent events, from discovering Ro's obvious challenge on Wednesday to the finale at the Shack yesterday, and the comments made by the other girls.

You get what you give. It's an interesting concept, particularly out of the mouths of the so-called *Sisters*. She wonders how they'd feel if this principle applied to them. Maz, with her competitive, entitled attitude, putting others down while simultaneously bragging about how amazing her own life is. Lettie, possibly the vainest, most narcissistic person Morgana has ever met, and a complete drama queen. Iris – sweet, kind, irritating Iris who'll do whatever it takes to keep the peace. Ro – but, no, disloyal, traitorous Ro has already got hers. She can be struck off the list.

Morgana's *Sisters*. The only people she can rely on and the people she hates the most. They might have chosen to conveniently forget the way they treated her when she first arrived in Avalon, aged twelve and knowing nobody, but she has not. She'd been scared and alone and all she'd wanted, all she'd *needed*, was to be accepted. But it was midway through Year Seven when everyone had already made their friends and formed their cliques, so what she got was a whole load of ridicule. She'd been treated like the outsider that she was.

Morgana lies back and delicately sips her drink, the knowledge that she's breaking yet another of her father's rules making the experience so much more enjoyable. The cold peach and guava juice slips down easily and she allows it to ease the lump that has appeared in her throat as she lets her mind wander back to that time, four years ago, when everything changed.

She can still remember how it felt when she and her mum drove through the town in the pouring rain. The sky was dark and sinister as they'd pulled up outside Gordon's lavish manor house. Pendragon Hall was located prominently on a piece of prime real estate in Avalon, with views of the sea on one side and the Tor on the other.

Morgana had known that there was something different about Avalon as soon as they'd stepped out of the car. Later, she learnt about the ley lines that ran underneath the town – pathways of energy beneath the earth – and the plethora of myths connected to the place, but back then she'd attributed the chills that ran down her spine, and the way the hairs on her arms stood on end, to the fact that her mother was suddenly introducing her to the man who was apparently her father. A situation that seemed to shock both Gordon and his wife, Alice, almost as much as it shocked Morgana.

Then her mother was gone, leaving her daughter at Pendragon Hall with empty promises to return as soon as she'd taken some time to *find herself*. Morgana overheard Gordon pleading with his wife, telling her that it wasn't his fault that his difficult one-night mistake couldn't cope with her daughter and what was he supposed to do if it was *his turn to deal with her* – they'd just have to *make the best of a bad situation*.

The *bad situation* being Morgana; that was made very clear by Alice. Morgana might only have been twelve but she wasn't stupid. The house was bigger and fancier than anything she'd had ever seen, but it was heavy with the burden of her existence and, as the days passed, she could see that weight pushing down on Alice like it was suffocating her.

Alice hated her. She hated that Morgana was Gordon's daughter. She hated that her precious son had a half-sister. Not that Morgana could blame her. Here she was, ruining their perfect dream life with her very existence. Alice was sublime – poised, graceful, well put together and never with a single hair out of place. Morgana didn't need a mirror to know that she looked as feral as she felt and was completely out of place in this museum of a house. She was her mother's daughter and Alice's opinion of *that witch* was that she, and therefore her daughter, was a wild, savage, dangerous creature.

Gordon and Alice enrolled Morgana at Avalon Academy, despite her protestations that there was no point because she wouldn't be there long. It was awful, but at least she had somewhere to go during the week. The weekends were the worst. Thirteen-year-old Art was always at the beach with his friends and, when Gordon asked him to take Morgana along, he offered some lame excuse about her being too young and made his escape. Gordon shrugged apologetically and told Morgana to keep herself busy, giving her a pile of cash and telling her to ask him for more when she needed it. Morgana hid most of the money under the mattress in her room, where her battered old canvas holdall sat in the corner, packed and ready to go the second her mother returned.

And she did her best to be invisible and stay out of

the way, she really did. Other than the beach, where she would only go when everyone else had left, the only thing to do in Avalon was climb the Tor or walk in the forest. On the one occasion that Morgana ventured past the treeline, the drop in temperature, the sinister caw of the ravens that were nesting in the trees, the feeling that she was being watched, made her scurry straight back out.

So that just left the town itself. And, as Morgana quickly discovered, Avalon was different. There was a regular supermarket, a few cafés and a library, but that's where the similarities to other places that she'd lived ended. Avalon was full of history and was built on ley lines. It prided itself on its mystical connections and was packed with shops filled with items to aid and enhance a person's spirituality. Morgana spent hours wandering around, examining crystals and spell bags, herbs and essential oils that smelt like her mother. Her only conversations during that time were with the shop owners, who were happy to share their knowledge of all things magick, including the healing properties of mugwort and how to cleanse crystals under a full moon. And then she walked into Brigid's Books, a tiny shop tucked away at the end of a cobbled alley, and everything changed.

Taking another sip of juice, Morgana remembers the conversation that started it all. She'd only gone inside to avoid the group of girls who were heading towards her on the street – Ro, Maz, Iris and Lettie, who were acting as if she didn't exist, as if they couldn't even see her. She'd hidden behind a bookcase, grabbing the first thing that came to hand as she pretended to browse the shelves.

"I didn't know we had that."

The voice came from behind, startling her. Morgana had spun round and come face to face with a woman. Her white hair flowed down her back, and Morgana couldn't tell if she was young or old. All she knew was that the woman was looking at her as if she knew who she was.

"Sorry?" The word had come out as a whisper.

"That." The woman nodded at the book in Morgana's hands, which had the title *Wytchcraft & Magick for Beginners*. "I haven't seen that book for many years. This is my shop and I had no idea that there was a copy on the shelf."

"Sorry," Morgana repeated, thrusting the book forward. "I was just— I mean—" She stopped, as the sound of the girls' laughter floated in through the open door. The woman glanced at the window and then strode across the shop floor, slamming the door closed so quickly that it seemed to Morgana as if she hadn't even touched it.

"It's a powerful book, that one." She leant against the shop counter. "Open it up. Choose whichever page feels right to you."

Morgana's heart was beating fast, but she did as she was asked, flicking through the pages until her fingers suddenly stopped.

"Now read it."

She stared at the words in front of her. The page was

entitled GET YOURSELF NOTICED and contained a list of ingredients followed by a set of instructions.

"I thought so." When she glanced up, the woman was smiling at her, looking pleased with herself. "It's been a while, but I knew it the moment I set eyes on you."

"What did you know?"

When the woman laughed, it sounded like rain lashing against the windows. "Is that relevant to you?" she asked, jerking her head at the book.

Morgana stared down at the page again and thought of the girls who looked through her every day. She nodded.

"Of course it is," murmured the woman. "The book knew you as soon as you walked in, as did I. Magick recognizes magick. Witch knows witch."

Morgana felt a strange warmth flood through her as she read through the steps of the spell, which suggested that she if she could lay her hands on six fresh yellow dandelion heads, a yellow ribbon, six drops of sandalwood essential oil and a teaspoon of honey, then all her problems would be over.

She'd never read anything like this before, but she felt suddenly certain she had the power to carry it out.

Witch knows witch.

"How much does it cost?" she asked quietly. Not that it mattered. She knew, more than she'd ever known anything, that she had to have this book.

The woman shook her head. "It's not for sale."

Morgana's fingers clutched tightly at the leather cover

and she glared at the shopkeeper, who laughed again, making Morgana shiver.

"You can't buy a book like that," she told Morgana. "It can only be gifted. Gifted by someone who knows it's worth and received by someone who is worthy of its power. It's yours."

Morgana had never been in the habit of accepting something for nothing, and she hadn't been about to start then.

"I have to pay you," she'd insisted. "I don't want it for free."

"Oh, there's a cost," the woman told her. "There is always a cost — that's non-negotiable. It's whether that is paid by you or by those around you, that's the thing. Take it, read it and I'll see you again."

She'd stated it like a fact. That was Morgana's first encounter with Brigid, but it certainly wasn't her last. And when the spell worked, and the girls at school stopped ignoring her and instead started calling her a weirdo and a loser, mocking her uncool hair, scruffy clothes and general lack of polish, she knew that she had to refine her powers and make them work for her. The pull that she felt to keep returning to the safe haven of the small shop was stronger than anything she had ever known.

Because Morgana had questions and Brigid had answers and there was work to be done. Taking some of the money from under her mattress, she'd exchanged it for a sense of control. It wasn't enough to be seen — she wanted to be accepted and that demanded more than just dandelions. She bought crystals, hiding the amethyst, quartz and tourmaline in an ornate wooden box. She spent hours and hours in her room, reading *Wytchcraft & Magick for Beginners* and feeling something shifting deep inside her. At Brigid's suggestion she purchased a journal.

"This will be your Book of Shadows," Brigid told her, wrapping it carefully in brown paper. "Every witch has one. It's like a diary where you can write down spells, charms and such. It's personal and must only be read by you, so keep it safe."

Morgana set about discovering how to harness the power that she could feel bubbling away inside. She memorised spells and learnt about charms and rituals. But what really fascinated her was the section on hexes – spells that curse.

"How come we never do any of these?" she'd asked Brigid, gazing at the instructions for a bad-luck hex.

"You shouldn't get involved in that sort of magick," Brigid had said. "Everything you put out into the universe will be returned to you by the power of three, and anyway, there's enough negativity in this world without us contributing to the pot." Then she had changed the conversation to her favourite topic – the ancient stories and legends of the women of Avalon. "Have I told you about Sibilla?" Brigid had asked, settling herself down on to the tall stool behind the counter. "She's someone you really do need to know about."

Morgana had continued to browse the shelves, hoping to find a book that might answer her questions about hexing if Brigid wasn't prepared to discuss it.

"She was one of the last women to be executed for being a witch, right here in Avalon," Brigid told her. "She had committed two crimes – well, four, if you count being a woman and being poor as criminal acts. But officially she was put on trial for selling apples and because one man claimed to have seen a raven flying into her bedroom window."

Morgana had peered round the bookshelf and stared at Brigid. "I mean, a raven flying into my room would be terrifying but it's not exactly illegal, is it? And what was the issue with the apples?"

Brigid sighed. "A child got sick after stealing one of her apples, and the parents decided that Sibilla had cursed him. And the man who witnessed the raven claimed that it was her witch's familiar. That was enough for the authorities to put her to death. They chained her to a rock in one of the caves down on the beach here and left her to drown."

Morgana selected a book that had a few chapters on hexing and went to the counter. "So she wasn't a witch, then?"

Brigid scanned the book and placed it into a paper bag. "Oh, she was a witch all right. But whether she was born a witch or the townsfolk made her that way with their accusations, nobody will ever know. Now she guards the entrance to the Otherworld – and if you see her, and she's offering you an apple, my advice is that you do not take it. Now, are you paying by card or cash?"

Morgana gave up trying to discuss hexes with Brigid. But the book she'd bought held a plethora of information, as did the internet – and Morgana was keen to learn.

She discovered that hexes were mainly used for revenge. The first step in seeking revenge is to identify the targets – a list of those to be hexed. Morgana already had a few people in mind and she wrote their names down in her Book of Shadows, starting with Alice, who only the day before had been overheard telling Gordon that his "illegitimate offspring" was an embarrassment and that he had better figure out a way to remove her from their perfect lives before she ruined everything. There was something deeply satisfying about writing down the names of those who hurt her and imagining the punishments that she would like to mete out to them as justice for the way they made her feel. The hex was supposed to offer her an outlet, a way for her to vent her anger. It was supposed to be about making herself feel better and making things fair. It was supposed to pay Alice back for being so cruel.

It wasn't supposed to end in murder.

On the night of the big storm she was the only one who saw Alice leave the house, unless you counted the raven who swooped through the skies above her. She was there, the wind and rain lashing at her face, reciting from the spell book under her breath:

You are the cause of pain and strife.

You cut me deep, your words a knife.

You are the cause of pain and strife.

I do not want you in my life.

Morgana had watched as Art's mother strode towards the path that led to the clifftops. She'd followed at a distance, not wanting to be spotted but instinctively drawn to whatever was about to happen. And she'd wished, with all her might, that Alice would keep walking and never come back.

She told herself afterwards that she hadn't really meant it — but she knew that wasn't the truth, even later as she struck through first Alice's name with her violet pen, and then Gordon's and Art's, because they had all paid a price.

If she'd needed confirmation that Brigid was correct, and that she truly was a witch, then this was it. When the sun rose the next day and Alice's disappearance was discovered, all hell had broken loose. In the chaos of organising search parties and offering rewards for information, Morgana had been forgotten. Shakily she had escaped the house and gone to seek Brigid's advice — only to find the bookshop closed and a for-sale sign swinging outside the entrance. She'd almost missed the envelope sticking out of the letter box, her name written in elaborate handwriting on the front.

Morgana had sunk down on to the doorstep and opened it up, tipping the contents out into her hands. The first thing to fall into her palm was a black crystal hanging from a silver chain. The second was an acorn and last was a single scrap of paper, scrawled with words written in Brigid's spidery handwriting.

> You are more powerful than you know, Morgana. Wear the obsidian to protect you from the negative forces that surround you. Place the acorn in your room — it will bring you good luck, power and much-needed wisdom. And always remember:
> When a raven is seen, the time is right.
> When a feather appears, the end is in sight.

So Brigid was gone and Morgana was alone again, but this time with the knowledge that the magick that felt so right to her could also be wicked. She vowed to only use her newfound magical powers on herself and keep other people out of it.

Regardless, Alice didn't return.

And Morgana's powers were written in the sand where Alice's body should have landed, but never did.

When her own mother sent a letter with the good news that she'd finally found herself and the less good news that she wouldn't ever be coming back, Morgana understood that this was the natural order of things: the give and take of the magick. *There is always a cost* — that's what Brigid had told her. She'd used her powers and Alice was gone — a mother for a mother.

She pushed the fierce rage, the third and final thing that her mother had left her with and that threatened to consume her, deep down inside, scared to give it full rein and she set her desires on being someone who was in control of her own destiny.

She used crystals to tap into the Earth's energy and she mixed herbs into tiny charm bags to ward off negativity. She read every page of *Wytchcraft & Magick for Beginners* and when she got to the end, she started again at the beginning, making notes in her own Book of Shadows. She spent hours in the sea, taking her energy from the sound of the waves and the feel of the water on her skin as she sank beneath the surface into beautiful silence. She imagined herself as popular and surrounded by people, and she spent that summer preparing. She watched movie after movie and made notes about what people found desirable. She watched YouTube videos made by gorgeous, glamorous girls and practised the way they spoke and moved and, by the time school started up again, Gordon's money had been put to good use.

Her hair was expertly cut into a choppy bob and her bedroom was filled with the most up-to-date make-up. Her skincare routine was a mixture of cleansers, serums, moisturisers and the dew that she gathered from the front lawn at dawn. Her clothes lined the railings and shelves of her walk-in wardrobe, along with the huge bulb-lined mirror where she could stand every morning and wonder at the shape-shifted creature before her with the perfectly sculpted eyebrows, the thick black eyeliner, the deep red lips and the ever-present black obsidian hanging from a silver chain round her neck.

Most importantly her heart was full of the belief that she could pull this off, that anything she decided to manifest would come true.

She had proof, after all.

On the first day of Year Eight she strode into Avalon Academy with the same focus as when she had watched Alice walk towards the cliffs, and with the same level of poise and control.

Nobody stood a chance, especially the girls who had made her life miserable the previous term. Morgana decided that they were hers, and it was so. As the most popular, beautiful, wealthy girls in Avalon, it suited her to have them in her group. But she would never trust them and keeping her true feelings hidden was a daily battle.

Now she drains the bottle of the final dregs of juice and sits back up. *You get what you give*. It's true; Morgana is living proof of that. She might present herself to the world as faultless and beautiful, but that's not the whole story. Not by a long shot. She's a master of putting on an act – and it's a necessity if she wants to keep the real Morgana Merrick hidden from view. Because her perfect façade hides a broken, cracked, rotten heart, and that's the price she must pay.

All she has to do is keep the raw, ugly truth of who she

is hidden behind the mask she wears every day. All she has to do is stop her ever-present rage from bubbling up to the surface and try to ignore the constant fear that the clock is ticking on her ability to keep it all together.

All she has to do is be perfect.

Candle Magick to Gain Popularity

You will need:

A toothpick

A saucer

A green candle, to symbolize friendship, abundance and success

5 drops of peppermint oil, for luck, energy and vitality

A sprinkle of cinnamon

I. Use the toothpick to carefully inscribe your name on the candle.

II. Hold the candle in your hand and state your desire to be more popular.

III. Put 5 drops of peppermint oil into a saucer and then sprinkle the cinnamon powder on top, allowing the aroma to enhance the power of the spell.

IV. Light the candle (safely) and let it burn – as it melts visualize your new life where you are surrounded by friends.

V. Extinguish the candle.

VI. Tip the oil and cinnamon outside, releasing it back to nature while thanking the universe for all that it provides.

VII. Enjoy your newfound success in all that you do.

CHAPTER 4

"Morgana, we're leaving!" Art's shout floats up the stairs. "If you're not downstairs in the next five seconds, then you're walking to school."

"Keep your knickers on." Morgana strolls out of the kitchen behind him, a perfect green apple in her hand. "I'm right here."

Art glances at her and scowls, Vivi hovering behind him anxiously. Art gives Vivi a lift too sometimes, which is a drag. "Do you honestly think you're going to get away with wearing your skirt that short? Mr Williams is going to have you in detention for a week if you walk into school looking like that."

"Looking like *what*, brother dearest?" Morgana raises an eyebrow. "Please do share your opinions about what I wear – I'm sure that Vivi and I are both desperate to hear your thoughts on what appropriate attire for the female should be, considering that you spend the vast majority of your life in shorts and most of the school sees your half-naked body on a daily basis."

Art shakes his head and walks towards the door. "Fair enough. It's none of my business. I'm just trying to stop you getting a reputation, that's all."

A reputation. Talk about sexist.

Morgana turns to Vivi. "Can you believe this loser?"

Vivi gives a nervous laugh. "I think he's just looking out for you."

Right. Morgana should have known better than to think Vivi might have an opinion of her own. Other than the fact that Vivi only ever wears baggy clothing, regardless of the weather, she is physically and emotionally incapable of saying anything that might contradict Art or Ginny or any of their annoying friends. She might only be their next-door neighbour but she's been in Art's life for ever and sometimes Morgana thinks that Vivi is more of a sister to him than she will ever be. They even wear matching necklaces – a silver spiral wave-shape pendant, which Vivi is fiddling with now. A wave. Pretty ridiculous, given that Vivi has never put as much as a toe in the water – she can't even swim. Just one thing in a long list of things that Vivi is incapable of doing, including displaying any level of backbone. It's tragic, it really is.

Morgana fixes her with an unblinking stare, as she

takes a big bite out of the apple before offering it towards Vivi. "Can I tempt you? Or are you scared that it might be poisoned?"

"Cut it out," barks Art. "We're leaving, with or without you."

Morgana saunters to the door, smiling sweetly as she passes Art. "My *reputation* has got nothing to do with my skirt length," she tells him. "You might want to remember that. Shotgun."

Art groans but still opens the door to let an uncomplaining Vivi fold herself into the back, while Morgana settles herself into the passenger seat and puts in her earphones. It might only be a ten-minute journey but she's had all the fun she's going to get out of Vivi for one morning and now she needs to focus her energies on preparing for yet another day of ruling the corridors of Avalon Academy.

There really is no rest for the wicked.

The bell for morning break rings, and all around the room kids leap up, grabbing their bags and racing to claim the best places to sit, chat and soak up whatever drama is occurring.

Morgana doesn't rush, instead choosing to slowly gather her belongings and then head out into the May sunshine at her own speed. The outside table and benches where she sits with the rest of the Sisters is sacred ground – nobody would dare to take their spot, not even any of the Year Twelves and Thirteens.

Except for today. As Morgana approaches the table, she can see that there is someone sitting there, and that someone is most definitely not a Sister. In fact, she's not a person that Morgana has ever seen at Avalon Academy before, and Morgana makes it her business to know everyone who attends this school. So she's a new girl. Morgana pulls out her gloss and swipes it across her lips, as Maz, Lettie and Iris fall into place around her.

And just when she thought today was going to boring.

Like a pride of lionesses, they stalk across the grass, their prey in their collective sight. Morgana is aware of the rest of Year Eleven watching this latest development; the last time someone tried to sit at her table uninvited was two years ago, and that didn't end well for that particular foolish student.

They reach the table and stand close to the intruder, who doesn't even look up. Her curly flame-red hair tumbles around her face as she leans over the table, her focus entirely on the book in front of her. Morgana waits for second longer than feels comfortable and then clears her throat.

Nothing.

Maz glances across at the rest of them, her face mirroring their confusion. Then she slams her hand down on the table. The noise echoes around the courtyard, making Iris jump, but the girl in front of them doesn't even flinch.

"What's going on?" whispers Lexie, as muttering

starts to spread amongst the other students. "Is it because Ro left? Do people think we're weak now that there's one less of us?"

"Get a grip," snaps Morgana, pushing Lexie out of the way and swinging her legs over the bench so that she's sitting opposite the girl. "Hey! I'm talking to you!"

She waves her hand in front of the girl's book and, finally, the red hair pulls up and a face appears. It's a normal-looking face, or it would be if it weren't for the eyes that gaze at Morgana and make her forget for a second why she's even there. She isn't sure that she's ever seen eyes that colour before – the deepest blue green that remind her of the sea when there's a thunderstorm.

"What's your problem?" demands Maz, sitting next to Morgana. "It's rude to ignore someone when they're talking to you."

The girl's eyes flick from Morgana to Maz, and then back again.

"Sorry," she says, her voice soft, although there's the sound of something tough behind it. "I didn't know you were talking to me. How can I help you?"

"You can't," snarls Maz. "We're here to help *you*, though. Move on – this is our table."

"Did you want to ask me something?" the girl says, still looking at Morgana, ignoring Maz completely.

Maz splutters and half rises from the bench, but Morgana shakes her head and holds one hand up, a warning to Maz to sit back down. She knows that actually she *does* want to ask this strange girl something, but she can't quite work out what it is. Those eyes make her feel like she's drowning – and she doesn't think she wants to save herself.

"Morgana," whispers Lettie from behind, yanking her out of the watery depths of the girl's gaze and back into reality.

"This is our table," murmurs Morgana. "You can't sit here."

The girl looks at her for another long minute and Morgana could swear that her eyes flash indigo blue. But then she nods, picks up her book and leaves. No apology, no excuse, no fight. She's just gone.

"Who the hell was that?" demands Maz.

"I have no idea." Lettie rolls her eyes. "But whoever she is, she'll think twice about sitting here again. The audacity of the girl. And did you see what she was reading? *The Magickal Properties of British Plants.*" She laughs. "We've got a baby witch in our presence, ladies – how on-brand for Avalon."

"That was a bit awkward," says Iris, looking worried. "I wish she hadn't sat at our table – it makes us look bad if people think we're not being friendly."

Now it's Maz's turn to laugh. "Iris, it makes us look bad if people think we *are* friendly." She pulls out her phone and starts swiping at the screen. "At least she gave us a chance to show everyone that we can't be messed with. I bet Avalon Asks is already buzzing with this."

Lettie and Iris take out their own phones and soon all

three of them are engrossed in the unofficial school gossip account. Morgana stands up and steps over the bench, heading across the courtyard to where the nerdy kids are always gathered by the door, ready for a quick escape back into school if anyone decides to target them.

"Who was that girl?" she demands, as she gets closer. They turn as a group, their faces registering horror that she's in their vicinity, clearly unsure how to handle this rare visit from the queen of Avalon. "Tell me who she is." For a person who doesn't *do* being ignored, Morgana's already at capacity for having to repeat herself for one day, and her voice is sharp.

"What girl?" asks the boy closest to her. "You're going to have to be a bit more specific."

"The one who was sitting at our table," Morgana snaps, and he takes a step back, bumping into one of the girls, Emily, who winces. "Red hair. Green eyes. Must be new."

The boy grins at her, and Morgana resists the urge to punch him in the face.

"Her name is Celeste," says Emily. "Someone said she used to live here but I don't remember her. She doesn't have to sit GCSEs or anything – apparently she's got special dispensation or something."

One of the other boys whistles. "God, I wish I didn't have to take exams. Williams told me the other day that I'll be lucky to even scrape a pass unless I start taking my revision seriously. Like that's going to help."

The first boy laughs and punches him on the arm.

"Maybe you should stop gaming every night until three a.m. and read a book or two? Exams start in one week, my guy."

"Celeste," says Morgana, letting the word slide around her mouth. "Do you know anything else about her?"

"Not really," says Emily, "although I did hear one weird thing about how she—" And then the one-minute bell rings and the rest of her words are swallowed up in the mob of people barging past them, desperate to avoid detention by getting into class before the sixty seconds are up.

Morgana steps to the side and waits for the rest of the Sisters.

"Where did you go?" demands Maz, as they join her. "What were you talking to that geek Emily about?"

"She told me that you've been blackmailing her to do your coursework. Which makes sense of how you've suddenly been getting the top grades that your parents pay you for."

Lettie giggles, and even Iris's mouth twists up into a small smile.

Maz flushes. "That – that's not—" she stutters, but Morgana has already swept away, flanked by the other two girls.

She's known about Maz's intimidation tactics with Emily for a while and has been keeping the information in her back pocket for a rainy day. She isn't entirely sure why she isn't telling the truth, but the one thing she does know, with complete certainty, is that she doesn't want to hear Celeste's name coming out of any of the Sisters' mouths.

She stalks inside the building. On the outside her face is its usual mask — calm, composed, impassive. But on the inside she is scanning the area, desperate for another glimpse of the mysterious girl who seems annoyingly, irritatingly, tantalisingly unbothered by Morgana's presence.

And that won't do.

That won't do at all.

CHAPTER 5

The sound of thumping bass thuds through the floor and Morgana slams her laptop shut in frustration. Maintaining her string of perfect grade nines doesn't happen by accident and, with the first exam only days away, she needs to focus on her revision. She's tried to ignore what's going on downstairs, but this is her house too and she's had enough.

The music increases in volume as she descends the stairs. She can hear them all out in the orangery and, by the sounds of it, the *informal gathering* that Art told her was happening has merged into a pool party. Slipping into the kitchen, she turns down the music by several decibels and then heads over to the fridge. She's debating the appeal of freshly cut melon over a pot of yoghurt when she senses someone standing behind her. As in, right behind her. She knows exactly who it is – there's only one person in Avalon whose smell makes every hair on her body stand on end in warning and repulsion.

"Morgana." His voice is quiet, but she can still hear it over the music. "How lovely of you to join us."

She forces herself not to react, instead reaching casually inside the fridge and randomly pulling out the first thing that her hand touches.

"I'm not joining you," she says. "I'm only here for a snack." Turning round, she shoots him a deliberately fake smile, realising too late that the "snack" in her hand is a block of butter.

Lance smirks. "Sure. Don't let me get in your way."

"Maybe move then." Morgana scowls at him, shoving the butter back in the fridge before slamming the door closed and stepping to the side, silently cursing herself for letting him get to her.

Lance moves across to the table, leaning against it with his legs crossed. The distance between them might have increased but Morgana is not feeling any more at ease. If anything, she's even more uncomfortable with the silence, which seems to hold her frozen in its grip.

"Nice PJs." He jerks his chin in her direction and she folds her arms across her chest, suddenly painfully aware of the cami top and shorts combo that she always wears to sleep in. The fact that he is only wearing a pair of surf shorts doesn't make the entire situation any better. There's a long beat while he gazes at her appraisingly and she tries to stare him out. Then the kitchen door flies open and Art tumbles into the room, dripping water on to the floor, followed closely by Ginny and Vivi, one in a bikini and the other clad in jeans and a hoodie.

"Dude!" he hollers. "What happened to you bringing us some more food?"

Lance holds Morgana's gaze for a moment, then looks away.

"I got delayed by your sister," he tells Art. "She was just telling me how she'd love me to give her some surf lessons."

"Oh, you totally should!" agrees Ginny, nodding enthusiastically. "Lance is a great teacher, Morgana – you'll pick it up in no time. He's amazing!" She flashes a perfect smile at Lance before stretching up to kiss Art on the cheek. "I mean, not as amazing as you, obviously."

"Obviously. Otherwise you'd be with him and not me, am I right?" Art flings his arm round his girlfriend and grins at Lance. "No offence, mate."

"None taken. As if I could go up against you!" Lance grins back and Morgana resists the urge to be sick in her mouth at this nauseating demonstration of bro-hood. "Anyway" – he turns his focus back to Morgana – "me and you, after school tomorrow at the beach. I'll have you standing up on the board in no time."

"Yeah, not happening," Morgana says. She glances at Art, who is now engaged in an obnoxious display of cutesy cuddling with Ginny, while Vivi shifts awkwardly. "Keep the noise down, OK? Some of us have got work to do."

"Yeah, yeah." Art waves a hand in the air, not even looking in her direction.

"Jeez, Art, it's worse than when your mum was still around," snorts Lance.

The room stills.

Morgana, who had taken two steps towards the door, freezes in position. Art disentangles himself from Ginny and looks at Lance in disbelief. Vivi's hand is pressed to her mouth and Ginny's eyes, wide and horrified, dart from one boy to the other.

Alice is *not* a casual topic of conversation around here, certainly not in the past tense, and Lance has messed up big time.

"I didn't mean—" The words stumble out of Lance's mouth, tripping over each other. "What I meant is—"

There's a moment of silence as one music track ends and then the next song starts up, loud, upbeat, and puncturing the tension in the room like a needle popping a balloon.

Art throws his arms in the air. "Last one in the pool pays for tomorrow's drinks at the Shack!" he yells and then they're all gone, a whirl of tanned limbs and long blond hair.

Morgana, alone again, allows herself to release the breath that she was holding and heads back to the fridge for the melon.

Lance is a loser and he isn't worth even one second of her time. She's got bigger things to think about, like ensuring that she nails this revision and gives herself enough time to plan the perfect outfit for Saturday night's beach party.

Heading back upstairs, she settles herself on to her bed and opens her laptop. She can still hear the faint beat of the music and the occasional screech of laughter that floats up through her open bedroom window, but those things don't really bother her now. Her thoughts have turned to the new girl and whether she'll be at the beach on Saturday.

It's been getting dull around here and it's about time that something happened to change the status quo. Morgana doesn't know why but there's a tiny voice in the back of her head telling her that Celeste might be the rip tide that pulls them all out of their comfort zones.

What the voice isn't telling her is whether this is a good thing – or whether the new girl's presence might end up engulfing them all.

Radiant Skin Potion

You will need:

250ml of rainwater

A jar

3 drops of pure rose oil

5 rose petals

I. Collect the rainwater in a jar.

II. Add the rose oil and mix well.

III. Sprinkle the rose petals on top.

IV. Leave the jar in a dark place for one week.

V. Once it is ready, lightly apply a few drops of the potion to your face each night before you go to bed.

CHAPTER 6

The flames of the bonfire flicker in the dusk and Morgana shivers. They might be having a particularly warm early summer but it is still only May and, once the sun starts to disappear below the horizon, the temperature is quick to drop.

"Have you seen what Vivi is wearing?" Lettie leans in towards the others, her voice conspiratorial. "Does she actually own anything that isn't shapeless and beige? *Mon Dieu!* I'd be embarrassed to leave the house looking like that."

"She literally doesn't care what she looks like," scoffs Maz. "I, on the other hand, spent ages getting ready for tonight. What do you think of my new dress? It costs a fortune and Mum will lose the plot if she finds out I'm wearing it to the beach, but it's lush, yeah?"

Morgana glances at the baby-pink mini tube dress that Maz is wearing. It looks expensive and she can see from the prominently displayed brand name that it probably cost more than most kids in Avalon receive in pocket money in three months.

"Yeah, it's fine," she tells Maz off-handedly, looking across the fire to where Art and his posse are engaged in an energetic game of beach rugby.

"Shall we join the game?" asks Iris, wrapping her arms round herself and inching closer to the fire. "I'm freezing."

Lettie scowls. "No way. I can't risk getting a broken nose – haven't I told you that I've got a modelling job coming up?"

"No, I don't think you've mentioned it," Maz tells her.

Lettie frowns. "Really? Well, it's a super-important—"

"God, of course you've banged on about it," snorts Maz, nudging Morgana in the ribs. "Like, fifty million times in the last week."

"What? Why would you—" starts Lettie.

"And it's so exciting, *isn't* it?" interrupts Iris, ever the peacekeeper, shooting a disapproving look at Maz. "I bet you're going to get super famous, Lettie, and end up on the front of *Vogue*."

Lettie shrugs, allowing herself to be appeased. "Maybe not *Vogue*."

"There's always the *Avalon Gazette*," snipes Maz. "Come on, let's go. I'll join Lance's team and you can all be with Art." She gives Lettie a meaningful look. "Surely that's enough to encourage you to play?" She stands and pulls Iris up to join her.

Lettie pouts, tossing her braids over one shoulder. "I'm not sure."

"It'll warm you up," Iris tells Lettie, who reluctantly pushes herself off the sand.

"Are you coming?" Maz looks down at Morgana.

"Not right now." Morgana shakes her head. "Got a headache. I might join you in a bit, though."

Morgana watches as the girls head down the beach and join in the game. Once she's sure that they are fully distracted, she turns her attention to the rest of the party.

It's packed, which isn't a surprise. Art's beach parties are renowned for their excellence and most of Year Twelve and Thirteen are present, along with a decent handful of Year Elevens, making the most of the last weekend before exams begin next week. The fire is encircled with kids roasting marshmallows and chatting, and further out there are groups of teenagers who would prefer to keep their activities in the darkness beyond the blaze. The rugby game has moved down to where the waves are lapping the sand and Morgana knows that it is only a matter of time before they progress to throwing each other in the sea.

What she can't see is any sight of Celeste, which is strangely disappointing.

Morgana picks up a handful of sand and lets it trickle though her fingers, trying to pretend that she didn't take extra care getting ready this evening just in case Celeste was here, because that would be ridiculous. All she wants to do is sit quietly, lose herself in the flames and let herself breathe properly for the first time in weeks.

"Morgana! Come and play!" The shout comes from down by the shoreline and when Morgana looks over, she sees Ginny waving at her enthusiastically. She raises a hand, indicating that she'll be there in a minute, and then rises to her feet. The last thing she has any intention of doing is getting involved in some stupid game that will almost inevitably result in her new silk vest top and sequin shorts getting trashed in the sea.

The evening air is cold against her skin as she walks away. For a second, Morgana regrets her decision and ponders whether it would be better to return to the warmth of the fire or to join the others. Then she hears a scream, followed by a splash, as Lettie is thrown unceremoniously into the water and her mind is made up. She heads down the beach, towards the cliffs and the one place where she knows she'll have some peace to think. The one place where nobody in the whole of Avalon would ever go. A place that the locals shun, where their children are banned from playing.

The sea cave used to be one of her favourite hang-out spots, back in that first summer when she arrived here. While the beach itself was the domain of Art and the rest of the surfers, nobody else ever ventured further along the cliff base to where the cave is hidden in between the rocks. The fact that this is the section of beach where Alice disappeared possibly had something to do with it.

Not that Morgana had been put off by that. Brigid had told her that the sea cave was where Sibilla was drowned as a witch; it made total sense that Alice would vanish on the cliffs above. There is a darkness in the cave that goes far beyond the lack of natural light.

Since Morgana reinvented herself, though, she hasn't been back. The town thinks it's evil and she's a nice girl now. She doesn't want anyone to associate her with the darkness. Although now it is that darkness that Morgana craves. Because in the dark she doesn't have to pretend. She can be herself, without the spotlight of attention forcing her to be everyone else's idea of perfect.

Approaching the entrance, she can feel her heart rate start to slow as her body begins to relax. A cawing sound makes her look up. There, perched on the rocks above the cave, is a raven. Morgana can see its nest. For a moment it seems to stare at her, its gurgling call reminding her of another time that she saw a bird like this, whirling in the sky above the cliffs as Alice stepped forward, buffeted by the storm.

When a raven is seen, the time is right.

And then her feet have decided for her, walking her forward and into the opening, letting the darkness swallow her whole. She moves confidently, her body remembering where it needs to duck to avoid banging her head on the low roof, and her arms out to the side. Her fingers trail along the damp walls as she steps across the sandy floor and towards the back of the cave until she's hidden from all view. She breathes in deeply, turning so that she's facing the entrance. She can feel the pressure of the cliffs pressing down around her and it feels like she's home.

She was right to come. She should never have stopped coming.

It is just as she remembered.

Dark — apart from the flicker of the bonfire far away down the beach.

Silent — apart from dripping and the distant sound of crashing waves.

Empty — apart from the figure who is looming towards her out of the shadows.

Morgana opens her mouth to scream but then a voice booms out in the darkness.

"It's only me. Surprise!"

"Oh for goodness' sake," mutters Morgana. "You scared me. What are you doing in here?"

"Looking for you." He steps forward and into her space, his silhouette cast by the light of the fire beyond the cave.

"Move out of my way, Lance." She pushes his arm but he doesn't budge and Morgana's stomach suddenly flips with nerves, which is ridiculous because it's just Lance, right? The boy she's known for four years. Her brother's best friend.

"Oh c'mon," he says. "One little kiss?"

Get out, girl. Go now.

Morgana doesn't know where the words are coming

from but for a brief second she thinks she sees the outline of a woman behind Lance, her arm outstretched as if to offer him an apple. She blinks and there's no one there.

"Let's go back to the others," she says coldly. "Stop being so pathetic."

He stares at her for a moment. "Your wish is my command, my lady."

Morgana takes a step in the direction of the entrance – and then Lance is pulling her towards him, pressing his lips firmly to hers.

It's only a second before she shoves him back, but it's a whole second too long. He laughs, as he stumbles against the cave wall.

"Oh come on, Morgana! Loosen up, will you?"

Shaking, she pushes past him, banging her shoulder on a sharp rock. As she runs along the beach, his laughter echoes in her ears. Even once she's a good distance away, even as she returns to the safety of the party, she can still hear it.

CHAPTER 7

The rugby game has finished. As Morgana makes her way back up the beach, she can see that everyone is gathered round the fire, sprawled on the sand in little huddles.

"Morgana!" Iris spots her approaching and waves. "Where were you?"

Morgana opens her mouth to reply but no words come out and then Lettie's eyes widen in surprise.

"Ooooh," she sing-songs. "I think we can all guess what *you* were doing."

"*Who* you were doing, more like," quips Maz, staring over her left shoulder.

Morgana turns her head and sees Lance standing a few feet behind her.

"A gentleman doesn't kiss and tell." He gives her a

salacious wink and then strolls round the fire to where Art is deep in conversation with Ginny and Vivi.

She watches him through the blazing driftwood. Fury races through her.

She's had enough. She's out of here.

"Where are you going?" calls Maz, but Morgana doesn't reply. She needs to get somewhere safe. That's all she can think about right now. She moves out of the light of the fire and stumbles up the beach, barely aware of the cold air that plucks goosebumps out of her skin.

As she starts up the wooden steps towards the Surf Shack, she feels a hand on her arm. She spins round and launches a punch.

"What the hell are you doing?" Art shouts, blocking her fist at the last second so that her knuckles only graze his cheek.

Morgana stares at him, blinking rapidly. She wonders about telling Art about what happened. But Lance is his best friend.

"I'm going home," she says coldly.

"Not on your own." He sighs resignedly. "I'll take you. Always a drama with you, isn't there?"

The car ride home is mostly in silence. Art makes a few pointed comments about the fun he's missing and Morgana stays quiet. She's torn between hurt and fury. As soon as they pull into the long circular drive of Pendragon Hall her fingers are clasping the door handle and she's out of the car almost before Art has stopped.

"You're welcome!" Art yells out of the driver's window.

Then the engine revs and he's gone, back to the beach and everyone else. Morgana gently closes the door behind her, too tired to even think about slamming it and seeing which treasured family memory of Art she can break. She kicks off her trainers, slowly making her way upstairs and into her bedroom, locking the door behind her when she's safely inside. Then she slumps down on to the thick cream carpet, the room lit softly by the lamps that she left on earlier when her only thoughts were on the party and who might be there.

Images crowd into her mind – the people who have wronged her.

Her mum, abandoning her at Gordon's house to pursue her own dreams.

Alice, blaming her for Gordon's sins.

Her father and Art, both wishing that her existence had stayed a secret.

Maz, Ro, Lettie and Iris. Four people who treated her like dirt because she didn't fit in.

Vivi, more a part of Art's life than she'll ever be. Always in the way.

Lance, who thinks he's untouchable.

In spite of all her efforts, nothing has changed since she came here to Avalon.

Morgana tips her head back and stares at the ceiling, feeling the luxurious pink room with its soft furnishings press in upon her in a way that feels heavier than the sea cave.

After everything she has done to shape-shift into the kind of girl that everyone wants her to be, she still isn't in control.

Everything about her is an illusion.

It's late when Morgana hears the front door open and the sound of footsteps coming up the stairs. They stop outside her locked door and she holds her breath.

"You OK in there?" whispers Art, rapping the door gently from the other side. "Morgana? Give me a sign of life."

"I'm fine," she mutters back, just loud enough for him to hear. "Go away."

"I've left you some crisps and a Coke," he says. "You left before the food." He waits for a minute, then she hears him heading away down the landing. His own door closes and Pendragon Hall is silent once more.

CHAPTER 8

"And then Williams told my mum that I need to stop spending my time, and I quote, *focusing on my extra-curricular activities* and start thinking about doing some revision." Lettie shakes her head in disbelief. "How rude is that? It's like he doesn't even want me to succeed."

"Have you actually done any revision, though?" Maz says. "Because you told us last week that you were completely stressed out and hadn't even started yet."

Lettie scowls. "That's not the point, is it?"

"I'm sure you'll be fine," Iris says soothingly. "And it's not like you need qualifications, is it? Not when you've got such a lucrative modelling career ahead."

Morgana gives Iris an appraising look. It's hard to take her seriously with the constant niceness. She'd like to think that Iris is hiding a dark, murky secret of her own beneath that cupcake exterior, but sadly she suspects that she actually *is* this boring.

"Do hand models make a lot of money then?" asks Maz slyly. "That surprises me."

Maz has been like this for days, ever since a slightly deflated Lettie admitted that her big modelling opportunity was, in fact, for a crafting magazine and that the only part of her being photographed was her hands.

"Why?" shoots back Lettie, instantly defensive. "It's a skilled profession that deserves a high salary."

"Skilled?" Maz snorts. "Literally anyone with fingers can do it. Look." She picks up her sandwich and offers it towards the group. "Ooh, I'm a model."

"Well, that shows how little you know," Lettie tells her. "You wouldn't get hired with those two-week-old nails for a start. Maybe think about booking in for a manicure, *Maz*. Even Vivi has got nicer nails than you, and that's saying something. *C'est tragique!*"

Morgana lets their babble wash over her. It's another sunny day and she's glad of the excuse to wear her sunglasses, the dark lenses giving her an added layer of protection. All she can think about is Saturday night and Lance. *How dare he?* Fury and confusion war within her. Her calm mask today is Oscar-worthy.

A flurry of kids emerge from the Year Eleven entrance and, as she watches, Celeste appears at the back of the group. She's alone, but she doesn't look lonely or awkward or self-conscious, or any of the things that most kids feel when they're on their own in a large group. Instead, she takes her time, pausing at the edge of the grass and looking around the courtyard, as if she's taking it all in. Her gaze lands on Morgana and for a few seconds they stare at each other from a distance. Celeste's blue-green eyes make Morgana feel like she's floating in the sea. The girl is captivating, hypnotic and Morgana is powerless to look away.

"I've got to return a book to the library," says Iris, the words barely registering. "Anyone want to come with me?"

"I will." Lettie stands up and grabs her bag. "I might see if they have any revision guides for English while we're up there, just to be on the safe side. Are you two coming?"

Morgana continues to just stand there, her focus entirely on Celeste.

"No." Maz sounds amused. "I think we're busy here. But good luck finding a revision guide that's going to help you pass an exam in two days' time!"

"Whatever," huffs Lettie, clearly still wounded. "See you both in maths. *Au revoir.*"

"Later," mutters Morgana. "Ow!" She turns to Maz, whose bony finger has jabbed her in the ribs. "What was that for?"

"Just seeing if you noticed," Maz says. "You seem a bit … distracted."

Morgana flushes and glances back at the grass, but Celeste is now walking away, her flame-red hair glinting in the sunshine.

"I don't know what you're on about," she tells Maz, who grins at her knowingly.

"Come off it, Morgana. We all know what went down with you and Lance at the beach on Saturday. You're quite clearly waiting for him to appear." She scoots along the bench and puts her arm round Morgana's shoulder. "So come on. Spill the details!"

Across the grass, Celeste has paused to speak to another girl. Morgana watches as they say something to each other and then the sound of laughter floats back on the air, Celeste's head is tipped back to expose a choker of green velvet round her long pale neck.

"You want the details?" she murmurs, not taking her eyes off Celeste. "OK. How about this? I can guarantee you that whatever Lance told everyone is a massive lie."

"Seriously?" Maz's voice is disbelieving. "So you two *didn't* kiss at the party?"

Celeste starts walking again and Morgana forces herself to focus on Maz. "There is no *you two*," she tells her. "*You two* suggests that something happened *between* us. That we both wanted it."

Maz frowns. "What are you saying?"

Morgana should shut up. She had no intention of having this conversation with anyone, let alone Maz. She especially shouldn't be having this conversation when her head is filled with fiery hair and ocean-deep eyes.

But maybe a girl needs to take a risk now and again.

"I'm saying that Lance kissed me when I didn't want

him to." She fixes Maz with a firm look. "I'm saying that he's a piece of dirt."

Maz's hand flies to her mouth. "Are you joking?" she breathes. "Like, is this for real?"

Morgana scowls at her. "Am I likely to joke about something like this?"

"You could report him," Maz tells her. "This is a big deal, Morgana. Are you OK?"

"I'm fine," Morgana tells her and then, when Maz gives her a doubtful look, she lets out a long sigh. "OK. So perhaps I'm not entirely fine. It was crappy."

The bell rings. All around them kids start heading back into school but neither of the girls move until the courtyard is empty.

"I can't believe it," Maz says, as they stand up. "What are you going to do?"

Morgana shrugs. "I don't know. But please don't tell anyone, OK?"

Maz pulls her in for a hug. "Of course not," she says, and Morgana can smell the cherry shampoo that she uses. "I'm here for you; you know that, right?"

Morgana gives her a quick squeeze back. "Thanks, Maz."

Maz releases her and picks up her bag. "Let's meet up at the Shack after school. One last get-together before exams begin. It'll cheer you up, yeah? I'll tell the others."

They walk together towards the building and, just as they reach the entrance, Morgana puts her hand on Maz's arm to stop her. "I mean it," she says. "I don't want anyone finding out about this. Not until I know what I'm going to do."

Maz returns her serious look. "I won't breathe a word. I promise. I'm just glad that you told me."

And, despite everything, Morgana realizes that she's glad too. Maybe opening up to Maz was the right thing to do. Maybe she can be a little bit honest now and again. After all, if she can't trust her Sisters, then who can she trust?

CHAPTER 9

Morgana is late getting to the Surf Shack, thanks to Mrs Kline, the head of Year Eleven and her insistence that Morgana, as their *model student*, lead a parent tour around Avalon Academy. By the time she arrives it's heaving with kids and she weaves her way through the crowd, searching for Maz and the others while keeping a careful lookout for any sign of Lance. Finally she spots Lettie and Iris in the queue for drinks and waves a hand to get their attention.

"We've got our usual table outside!" shouts Iris. "Go and defend it with Maz – we'll get you a smoothie. What do you want?"

"Coconut and mango," she calls back. "Thanks!"

They smile at her and she grins back, feeling an unfamiliar sense of camaraderie wash over her. Perhaps she's been too hard on them all. Maybe she needs to leave the past in the past and accept that these are her people, there for her when things get tough.

She pushes her way towards the raised decking at the front of the Shack, spying Maz at the coveted table on the far side near the railing, deep in conversation with Ginny and Vivi. Morgana glances left and right, confirming that neither Art nor his best friend are anywhere to be seen. The coast is clear. She weaves between tables of loudly moaning Year Elevens and Thirteens, stressing about exam pressure, to Year Twelves who look distinctly relieved to be having a year off.

As she gets close, she opens her mouth to announce her presence, but then Maz's words buzz their way into her ears and she darts behind one of the potted palm trees that the Shack has dotted around instead.

"I told Morgana that I couldn't believe it," Maz says. "What I *should* have said was that I *don't* believe it. There's a difference."

"I don't understand why she'd even say something like that." Ginny's voice is affronted, as if she's the one who's been accused. "We all know Lance. He's not like that."

"Right?" Maz snorts. "I bet he's not even interested in her."

There's a pause and Morgana holds her breath. Then, to her surprise, Vivi speaks up.

"Lance *did* tell us that they kissed." She pauses to sneeze. "Perhaps Morgana is telling the truth. Maybe something did happen?"

"Exactly!" Maz sounds triumphant, as if she's just been proven right. "That's what I'm saying. She's always leading Lance on – we've all seen it. If they kissed, it's only because Morgana was asking for it. When have you ever known anyone to get Morgana Merrick to do something that she doesn't want to do?"

They think she was *asking for it*? What the hell? Do they even know what they're suggesting? Are they going to start discussing what clothes she was wearing next, and blame her for looking so good that he couldn't help what he did?

Her friends think she lied about what Lance did.

They think that it's her fault and they're completely letting him off the hook.

This is wrong on a whole new level. Morgana clenches her fists and tries to pull air into her burning lungs.

"That's an excellent point." The amusement in Ginny's voice oozes around the palm tree and thickens the air. "It's way more likely that she instigated the whole thing, not the other way round. Do you think we should say something to Lance about it? Like, maybe warn him?"

"No." Maz is casual. "It's nothing. She'll get over it. You know Morgana – she'll have moved on to the next thing before we know it."

"The next boy, you mean?" Ginny chuckles. "I asked Art about that but he shut me down – apparently he wasn't prepared to discuss his sister's dating habits!"

"Well, why should he?" says Vivi, again surprising

Morgana. She sends her unlikely champion a silent *thank you*, shifting slightly to the side so that she can watch the girls while remaining hidden behind a palm frond. "And I can't believe you think she was leading Lance on."

"Oh come on," says Maz. "Morgana has kissed loads of boys. She just doesn't talk about it."

It's not loads.

It's one.

And that was without her permission.

"Enough about Morgana," Maz says. She sniggers. "How about you, Vivi? Hooked up with anyone lately?"

There's a moment of silence and then both Maz and Ginny burst into peals of laughter.

"I'm sorry, Vivi," splutters Ginny. "Don't take this the wrong way but the idea of you getting with anyone is…"

"Right?" Maz laughs again, while Vivi looks hurt. "You're destined to be a cat lady."

"I like cats," mutters Vivi, flushing a deep red. "But that doesn't make me a cat lady."

"Whatever. Hey, over here!" Maz issues an ear-splitting whistle that makes Morgana flinch and retreat back out of sight.

"God, that queue was insane." There's the sound of a tray clattering on to the table and Morgana hears Iris and Lettie pulling chairs across the floor. "Where's Morgana? She was headed out here…"

It's time to move. Ducking low, Morgana scurries across the decking, making it round the corner before anyone can see her. For the second time in the last few days, she is retreating, but this time there is a difference.

As she walks home, her rucksack bouncing up and down on her back, she can feel it growing. By the time she enters the driveway of Pendragon Hall, her heart is pounding like the crashing of the waves and, when she slams the front door behind her, relishing the sound of smashed glass from another broken picture, she's burning up.

On Saturday she was ice: frozen and numb. Today, she is fire.

This heat is fierce.

This burning is a raging inferno.

These flames are out of control.

For four long years she has bent herself into a shape that others will find attractive, too afraid of what she might be capable of if she lets her rage bubble up. She's pushed down her feelings and dampened her spirit and made herself tame.

And now it's time for all that to change.

Morgana is going to add as much fuel to the fire as she possibly can.

Self-Esteem Chalice Spell

You will need:

1 stick of frankincense incense

A glass or goblet (as a chalice)

1 pink candle, for love

A key, to access hidden things

A paper or card disc of a size that will fit on top of the chalice

3 tablespoons of rainwater (tap water will do in an emergency)

A few sprigs of lavender, for happiness and tranquillity

2 tablespoons of apple juice

I. Light the incense and the candle (safety first – put them in the correct holders and never leave them unattended).

II. Write your name on the disc, followed by three hearts.

III. Add the lavender to the chalice, saying:
<u>For all that I am, and all I can be.</u>

IV. Add the key, saying:
<u>Unlock my secrets and show them to me.</u>

V. Add the water and apple juice, saying:
<u>As the water flows endless and the apple is raw,</u>

VI. Hold the chalice in both hands as you gaze into the candle and say:
<u>Show me my beauty – let me love myself more.</u>

VII. Extinguish the candle and the incense stick and go about your day, remembering that you are the most precious thing in the universe.

CHAPTER 10

Once in her bedroom, Morgana locks the door and goes to her bed, dropping to her knees to retrieve the box from underneath. Pulling it out, she dusts off the top and then climbs on to her duvet, sitting cross-legged with the box in front of her. She hasn't looked at the contents for almost four years; she hasn't needed to. But now she lifts the lid and gazes at the items inside. The items that allowed her to change everything. To transform herself. She simply used the tools and methods that women have used for centuries.

Magick.

Not the Harry Potter kind – she's not delusional. No, Morgana found something way more powerful and effective than goblins and mythical creatures. Her own mind.

The book is lying right at the top. Morgana picks it up,

holding it gently. She traces over the tree of life embossed into the soft leather cover before opening it up and reading the title page.

Book of Shadows – her journal, recipe spell book, grimoire, map.

Morgana flicks through the pages, smiling at the drawings inside – labelled pictures of an amethyst, a spell for feeling less lonely and several pages devoted to moon magick, alongside journal entries. She pauses at one that is only eight words, written in her childish writing and then quickly skims past.

I just want to know who I am.

There might come a time when she wants to relive those early weeks when her mum left, but that time is not now. Instead, she turns to the back page and the list.

~~Alice~~
Mum
~~Gordon~~
~~Art~~
Ro
Lettie
Iris
Maz

Picking up the violet pen that is inside the box, she gives it a shake to loosen the ink and then takes off the lid, striking a neat line through Ro's name. Her fate was sealed by Morgana alone, and not magick – but with the same end result. The traitor can join Alice, Art and Gordon as people who have been dealt the cards that they had coming. Alice is gone and Gordon and Art's lives were for ever changed by her loss. Ro betrayed Morgana and now has no friends. It's harsh but only fair.

Then, neatly, carefully and with complete focus, she adds Lance to the end of the list, feeling a thrill of anticipation and excitement as she sees it next to Maz's name.

It is written. It cannot be taken back.

A bag of crystals is next out of the box, followed by a small bottle of rose oil and a bundle of lavender. A tiny acorn. Small inconsequential things on their own, however Morgana knows that they worked before and they can work again.

This time it's different, though. Four years ago, she was asking the magick to help her become someone she was not. Someone perfect.

Now, like the waxing moon, it's come full circle. As far as almost everyone else is concerned, Morgana Merrick has it all.

Turning to a fresh page, she starts to write.

Like Maz said, nobody makes Morgana Merrick do anything. That's what everyone thinks, anyway. Her own friends don't believe her. She's destined to be either a victim or a villain and there is no way in this universe that she will ever allow herself to be a victim. So Lance hasn't given her much of a choice.

Villain it is.

CHAPTER 11

"How was your English exam?"

Art stuffs another slice of pizza in his mouth and looks over at Morgana. It's been just over two weeks since Gordon left on his business trip and they have settled into something that resembles a routine, taking it in turns to order in food every evening and deciding on a film that they can watch on the gigantic home cinema. Art has even agreed not to host any *informal gatherings* on a school night. Which means it should just be the two of them.

Or it would be if Vivi wasn't constantly hanging around. Morgana can just about tolerate her, but she's not exactly scintillating company.

"Fine." She looks back at the screen, keen to avoid the

sight of over-chewed pepperoni in his half-open mouth. "It went well."

It's the truth; although it almost wasn't. When Morgana opened the English Literature paper in the school hall that morning and saw that the first question was about the three witches from *Macbeth*, it took all her concentration not to let her mind wander to her Book of Shadows and the spell that she wrote out last night. Thankfully the months of revision paid off and she was able to write about their prophecies and the way that Shakespeare used them to advance the plot without too much effort.

"When's your next one?" asks Art. "God, this movie is terrible. If the dude is that scared of heights, then why would he decide to climb a mountain? It's not even believable acting – I've seen Lance when he's up somewhere high and the guy can barely speak, he's so freaked out."

Morgana smirks. "Lance is scared of heights?"

"Terrified." He glances at Vivi and Morgana. "Don't tell him I told you that, by the way. He works really hard to hide it. Unlike this loser."

"We can watch something different," Vivi says quickly, as desperate as ever to please.

"I've got three more exams before the end of the week." Morgana yawns and stretches her arms above her head. "I'm going to head up now – I want to read through my notes again and then I've got to get some sleep."

"Are you OK?" Art says. "I heard that Maz has been saying some stuff about you."

"You mean that Vivi, our friendly neighbourhood busybody, told you." She raises an eyebrow at Art.

"I wasn't trying to cause trouble." Vivi looks worried. "I just thought he should know. It's not fair what Maz has been saying."

Morgana ignores her. "I'm fine."

Art mutes the television and shifts round so that he's properly facing Morgana. "You've got a lot going on with exams and everything. It must be kind of hard doing all this without…"

He pauses, and Morgana raises an eyebrow. "Without what?"

"You know." He starts fiddling uncomfortably with the wave pendant that dangles from his neck. "Without any family of your own."

Without any family of your own. It hurts more than it should. Morgana knows Gordan and Art aren't exactly thrilled by her presence, but even so — Art could at least *pretend* they're family.

"It's fine." Morgana stands up, tucking her white strands of hair behind her ear. "Family is overrated. You should be the expert on that."

Art frowns up at her. "What do you mean?"

She throws him a smile as brittle as splintered glass. "Let's see. Gordon cheated on Alice with my mother when you were a baby and didn't even tell her I existed until I turned up on your doorstep. Then Alice went and—" She stops, her words gripping the edge of a cliff for dear life, trying to prevent themselves from plummeting over and never being able to be taken back.

"My mother went and *what*?" Art is standing up now too, his eyes flashing with something that is either fury or fear – Morgana knows only too well how much those two emotions love to masquerade as each other. "My mother is missing – everyone knows that. She'll be back one day, when the time is right."

Everyone knows that's the story that Art insists on telling and that Gordon Merrick allows him to believe. It doesn't mean that it's the truth, though. Not that Morgana is keen for the *actual* truth to come out.

"It doesn't matter," she says, backtracking. "The point is that you're no better off than I am, so don't be giving me any fake *poor abandoned child* chat, OK?"

"I've still got my mum and my dad," Art snaps. "And this is my home."

"Sure." Morgana starts walking towards the door. "And when did Gordon last give you anything that wasn't a deposit into your bank account?"

"That's a crappy thing to say." Art's voice is quiet. "And, for the record, my life was fine until you arrived and destroyed everything."

Morgana spins to face him, her features taut with anger. "I didn't *ask* to be left here. I didn't *ask* for *any* of this. You're just like everyone else – hiding behind an act because you're too scared of who you really are." She stalks towards him, and it feels like her skin is on fire. "Well, I'm not scared, Art. Not any more."

He holds his hands up, backing away slightly. "OK, OK, I get it."

"No. You don't." She glares at him, her heart pounding. "You can't possibly *get* any of this. You can't understand what it feels like to have to be one hundred per cent perfect every single second of every single day and god forbid that you mess up because there are no other chances. Not when you've already used them all up."

"Whatever." Art slumps back down on to the sofa. "I don't have a clue what you're talking about and I don't want to argue with you. Just don't ever talk about my mum and dad like that again, OK?"

Morgana exhales, suddenly aware of Vivi staring at her with her mouth wide open. Any fight rushes out of her body. He's right. Alice was his mother. Gordon is his father. She's allowing her wrath at the others to be directed at him.

"And I shouldn't have said that about you not having any family," Art continues. "It was stupid. We have each—"

"Just forget it," interrupts Morgana. He doesn't mean it, anyway. "I'm going to bed."

"Morgana." Art sighs heavily. "Can we talk about what Maz said? This story that Lance—"

But she's gone, up the stairs and back to the safety of her room with the door locked behind her. Art isn't her target and there are other people who need to be dealt with.

Not Lance – not right now. She's not going after him immediately. He deserves something special and she's not quite ready for that yet. Besides, he'll keep. Right now, she has someone else in mind.

Dusk is falling. As she closes the curtains, a flash of blue black catches her eyes from the tree just beyond the small balcony outside her window, but when she looks again, there's nothing there. Still, she can't escape the feeling that something is out there, watching, waiting.

Is it waiting for her? Or for someone else?

Opening the Book of Shadows, she turns to the journal entry and spell that she wrote yesterday, adapting a similar spell from *Wytchcraft & Magick for Beginners* to suit her needs. It required a few ingredients that she didn't have, but a quick trip to the shops on the High Street after school has dealt with that. She's already *borrowed* Gordon's antique silver candlesticks from the mantelpiece in the dining room and created a shrine on top of her chest of drawers, with her crystals and the acorn from Brigid laid out in an intricate pattern in the centre. Her newly purchased indigo candles are in place, the colour chosen for its connection to justice, and now she strikes a match, breathing in the smell of sulphur as the candles flicker into life.

Breathe in – planting her feet firmly on the floor and letting the universe's energy flow up through her legs, body, arms, neck, head.

Breathe out – eyes closed, allowing the energy to flood

out in a stream of white light, casting a protective circle all around her.

Breathe in – feeling the force of the earth working, emboldening, empowering.

Breathe out – releasing any tension. Focusing her mind.

The book lies open on the shrine, propped up so that she can see it clearly. Morgana opens her eyes and moves slowly, mindfully, carefully, following the instructions for the freezer spell that she wrote yesterday, letting the ritual focus her mind on what it is that she really wants.

She thinks about how it felt to hear Maz betray her confidence.

She thinks about the millions of girls who have been accused of *asking for it* and the other girls who were their loudest denouncers.

She thinks about the stories that Avalon is built upon and the way that its women are written as either perfect or evil, saint or sinner – with nothing in between.

She lets her mind stretch out, beyond the walls of her bedroom, beyond the confines of Pendragon Hall. She gazes at the photograph that is propped against the candlestick and she holds the fire agate crystal that she bought earlier in her hand, repeating her mantra under her breath.

Keep my name out of your mouth.

Shut-Your-Mouth Freezer Spell

You will need:

Photo of the person who is doing the gossiping (optional)

Fire agate crystal, for power and protection

A glass jar

9 cloves, to block out darkness and banish gossip

Salt water, to make the words turn bitter in their mouths

I. Ground yourself. Allow the energy of the universe to fill your veins.

II. Visualize the person who you wish to stop spreading lies and gossip about you (the photo helps with this).

III. Hold the crystal in your hand and state the following intent:
<u>My name is my own – it belongs only to me.</u>
<u>I call on the powers of the deep briny sea.</u>
<u>Air to the east and fire to the south,</u>
<u>Keep my name out of your mouth.</u>

IV. Place the photograph inside the jar and add the cloves. Then fill the jar with salt water, making sure to tighten the lid.

V. Put the jar into the freezer (make sure it won't be disturbed). The spell will silence the gossip's words and freeze them out of your life.

VI. Keep the fire agate close by you until the magick is done.

CHAPTER 12

The sand is warm beneath her. Morgana stretches out her legs, admiring her freshly painted toes – her treat to herself after the first week of exams – and tries to ignore Art, Ginny and Lance, who have given up on attempting to find a decent wave and instead are sitting astride their boards, feet dangling in the water, deep in conversation. She'd far rather be out there letting the sea wash over her than stuck here with the *Sisters,* but she never swims when there are other people around. The way she feels when she's submerged beneath the waves has got nothing to do with anyone else.

"I'm going to ask Art for lessons." Lettie stares out to sea. "I think I'd be *une naturelle.*"

It's probably true. Lettie is irritatingly good at most things she attempts, other than schoolwork.

Maz follows her gaze and laughs. "I can guess why. But you might want to remember that he's got a girlfriend already. And I'm not sure that he's going to want to give up all of *that*" – she waves her hand in the direction of Ginny – "for someone whose best attributes are their hands. Then again, I might be wrong."

"Shut up, Maz," snaps Lettie. "I said that I wanted surf lessons with Art, not to get down and dirty with him."

"Gross," mutters Morgana. "Can we not discuss this, please?"

Maz laughs again and Morgana resists the urge to throw sand in her face. She checked the spell jar this morning and the liquid still hadn't frozen. She's wondering now if she might have been a bit overzealous with the amount of salt that she added to the water.

"Why haven't you ever learnt to surf?" Iris rolls over on to her stomach and looks at Vivi. "You must get bored sitting here watching them all the time?"

"I don't mind," Vivi says, shielding her eyes with her hand against the bright afternoon sun. "I'm a bit nervous and seawater can make my skin break out – but I still might learn. I haven't decided yet."

"Right." Maz shakes her head. "You've lived in Avalon your entire life – if you've not surfed yet, I don't think you ever will. It's pretty obvious that you're never going to be a wave warrior. You'd have to stop being scared and allergic of *literally everything* first."

"Maz, that's not very kind." Iris's voice is admonishing.

"People have different talents. Vivi might not be a surfer but I'm sure there's something else that she's good at."

"Are you?" Maz plants her hands in the sand behind her and leans back, an appraising look on her face. "How intriguing. And what do you think that something might be?"

Iris frowns in confusion. "Well, I don't know, do I? I've never actually— Oh, shoo! Go away, you freaky thing."

Lettie laughs. "Vivi *is* a bit of *une petite freak*."

"I didn't mean Vivi!" Iris scoots across the sand. "I was talking to the weird crabs."

Morgana cranes round to look. Sure enough, four or five crabs are scuttling across the sand, headed straight for Vivi, who puts her hand down and lets them scurry across her skin as they continue their journey down to the water.

"Oh my god, Vivi's got crabs!" crows Lettie. "Amazing."

Vivi frowns. "What do you…?"

"Never mind," says Lettie, flashing a grin at Maz.

Morgana sighs quietly and debates whether she can get away with leaving early. Taunting Vivi is a bit like kicking a puppy and, for or some reason, it's starting to bother her. It would be OK if Vivi ever fought back, but all she ever does is sit there looking a bit sad.

"Vivi?" Maz turns to look at her. "Can you shed any light on your mystery talent? You must do something other than hang out with your cat."

A red flush starts to creep up Vivi's neck and suddenly Morgana has had enough.

"Hey, Maz?" Her voice is deceptively soft. Unlike her Sister, she doesn't need to use brute force to put someone down. "I heard you've been talking about me to some of the others. Behind my back."

Maz's head whips round so fast that Morgana swears she hears her spine creak.

"What? No. What are you on about? I haven't said anything. Who told you that?"

Her panic is palpable. The other girls are watching with interest, although Vivi, predictably, is looking anxious.

"What was it?" asks Lettie, ever ready to sniff out a drama and keen to pay back Maz for her earlier comments. "What did she say, Morgana?"

Vivi sits up straighter, nervously lifting her chin. " I don't think we should talk about this."

"Do you want to tell them, Maz?" Morgana raises one exquisitely groomed eyebrow. "Or shall I?"

Maz stares at her in horror. "I don't know who said anything to you, but whatever they said is a lie."

"Oh, really?" Morgana frowns. "How do you know, when I haven't said what it was yet?"

"I'm sure that Maz would never say anything bad about you, Morgana," says Iris, once again trying to smooth out any hint of trouble.

"Right?" Morgana smiles at Iris. "Except she did. Maz accused me of being a liar."

"I didn't," splutters Maz. "What I said was—"

"Yes?" Morgana looks Maz straight in the eyes. "Do tell us what you said."

Maz swallows and Morgana smiles. This part is always the most delicious.

She waits for a few beats, the other girls holding their breath in anticipation of a showdown. And then, when she sees that Maz is about to crack, she reaches out one delicate hand and places it on Maz's arm.

"Let's forget about it," she suggests. "After all, maybe it was all a misunderstanding and you didn't actually say that I was *asking for it* when Lance kissed me against my will."

Maz gulps.

"No, she did," mutters Vivi. "That's exactly what she said."

Iris looks at her with concern. "That's awful, Morgana."

"I'm so sorry, *ma soeur*," says Lettie. Then she turns to glare at Maz, her beautiful face creased in anger. "That's not exactly Sister code, is it? What happened to girls supporting girls?"

What happened *to it?* Morgana thinks. *It was never there to begin with.*

"I didn't mean it that way." Maz looks at Morgana beseechingly. "You have to believe me."

"I don't *have* to do anything apparently," Morgana tells her. "*Nobody makes Morgana Merrick do anything.* Or did you forget that part?"

There is silence.

Morgana stands up, brushing sand off her legs. "I'm going to get a drink," she tells the group. "I'll be back in a bit."

The queue is out of the doors of the Shack but she doesn't mind. Joining the end, she pulls out her phone and starts swiping through her various accounts, noting with amusement that Avalon Asks has just posted a poll asking kids to vote on who is the most influential girl in Year Eleven, from a choice of two. Her and Maz. She can't see who created the post – pretty much the whole school know the login details and anyone can add anything. She suspects this is Lettie, trying to stay relevant. What she *can* see, as she shuffles closer to the serving counter, is that her name is already leaping ahead, putting her in a great position to win the Most Popular Girl award that is always presented at the final beach party of the school year.

Poor Maz. Morgana's heart breaks for her, it really does.

Still smirking, she pockets her phone. And then someone appears at her side.

"Hi."

It's the new girl. Celeste. Standing right beside her.

Morgana instinctively smiles, her pulse speeding up as those blue-green eyes hold hers.

"Is it OK if I push in?"

Yes.

It's OK. Very OK.

Let's stand here for a while, just the two of us, and let everyone else fade into the distance.

"Thought I'd join you." Lettie's voice cuts through the moment as she makes an unwelcome appearance. She scowls at Celeste. "Um, are you pushing in?"

"Yes. Sorry." Celeste doesn't sound remotely apologetic.

Morgana quickly adjusts her face into a frown. The arrival of Lettie means that she has to deal with this the right way. The only way. She needs to put this girl in her place.

"There's a queue for a reason." She makes sure that her voice rings out, calm and steady with a hint of danger. "Join the back."

"Fine." The girl grins at Morgana. "I'm Celeste, by the way."

"Great." Morgana bares her perfect white teeth in a wolf smile, hating herself as she does it. "I'm Morgana – and you're *in* my way."

"I know who you are." Celeste tilts her head to one side, as if she's trying to work something out. "I'm not sure that you do, though."

And then she's gone, moving lightly through the packed Surf Shack and outside.

"That girl has issues," says Lettie, glaring at her retreating back.

"What can I get you?" asks the kid at the counter. Morgana grabs a bottle of water, waves her card at the machine and dashes out of the Shack, but by the time she reaches the decking area, there is no sign of anyone with a beautiful, irritating mouth, fiery-red hair and eyes that look as fathomless and dangerous as the Mariana Trench.

CHAPTER 13

The alarm wakes Morgana early on Saturday morning. Cursing, she silences the noise and rolls over, determined to go back to sleep. But for some reason her throat is really hurting and her head is full of thoughts that don't want to be quiet and so she finally, reluctantly, succumbs to the reality of being awake. She really hopes that she isn't getting sick – she doesn't have time for that now.

Pushing back the duvet, she walks across the room and pulls back the curtains, remembering the sensation of being watched the other night and half expecting to see the bird perched on the railing of her balcony. *When a raven is seen, the time is right.* But there's nothing there. She grabs her revision books, returns to bed, and spends the next few hours going through her notes for the history exam that is scarily close, while sipping water to try to ease the pain in her throat that seems to have manifested overnight.

By ten o'clock she's done. Throwing down the books, she picks up her phone and starts skimming through her various social media accounts, ready for some distraction that is unrelated to chronologies and key events and enquiry skills. Iris has posted a cute photo of them all from yesterday. Her own picture – one of her sunglasses and bottle of water on the sand with *#beachlife* – has already had several hundred likes.

Her phone pings as a new poll appears on Avalon Asks and she swipes to the page, wondering what insightful question will be being asked of the school population today. Recent *asks* have featured Avalon's favourite ice-cream flavour, choice of celebrity crush, hottest girl in Year Eleven (she won, obviously), which teacher should get fired and who would win in a fight between Art and Lance (it was a dead draw).

Today's poll looks at first glance to be just as inane. As usual, it's been posted anonymously and the title is LOADED OR EXTRA LOADED. Beneath that is a photograph of Maz and, as Morgana looks at the screen, the votes start pouring in.

Loaded
Extra Loaded
Extra Loaded

She rolls her eyes. This is pathetic, even for Maz, who has quite clearly posted this herself to boost her own status. She's always going on about how much money she has and how much everything costs. Morgana has been tempted on several occasions to enquire as to why she hasn't attempted to buy herself a personality if she's so minted, but always stops herself at the last moment. Her power comes from a subtlety that Maz is incapable of and she rarely allows herself to reveal her true thoughts, instead cultivating the situation so that others will say it for her.

Some might call that manipulation. Morgana calls it smart.

Maz has good timing, though; Morgana will give her that. Saturday morning, before anyone has the energy to face the day, is the perfect time to get everyone's attention.

She looks back at her screen. Eighty-nine per cent of the voters have chosen *Extra Loaded* and Morgana idly wonders what purpose Maz is hoping to serve with this ridiculousness.

Then there's the *ping* of a notification on Avalon Asks and Morgana checks it. Her eyes widen in shock. She sits up in bed and holds the phone closer to her face, trying to get her brain to register what she's seeing. Because this cannot be real.

Please, universe, let this be real.

It's a video. Only a short clip and clearly filmed from a distance, but the image is crystal clear. Morgana hits the replay button once, twice, and then a third time. The view counter underneath indicates that she is not the only person enjoying this surprising Saturday entertainment. And then the comments start to roll in.

> *What the hell?*
> *Is that Maz?*
> *Is she doing what it looks like she's doing?*

On the screen, Maz is casually skimming through a rack of clothes in what is instantly recognisable as one of Avalon's high-end boutique stores. She selects the baby-pink mini tube dress that she was wearing at the beach party last week and holds it up, posing in the full-length mirror as she admires it against herself.

And then, with a furtive glance over her shoulder to check that nobody is watching, she rams it inside her bag with one slick movement, before moving on to look at another item of clothing.

"Oh. My. Word." Morgana watches the footage again, just to be one hundred per cent sure.

Maz stole the dress.

And now the comments are flowing in faster than she can read them. Morgana watches in awe as Avalon Academy rips Maz to pieces with their words.

> *Thief*
> *Fake*
> *Loser*

Fraud

Phoney

Scum

They keep coming, like a relentless tide. There's no stopping it – not that Morgana has any desire to do that. Instead, she leans back against her pillows and keeps reading, each word warming her from the inside.

They hate Maz. They hate the way she's always made them feel inferior. They hate the way she's always flaunted her supposed wealth – and now they despise her for being a goddam hypocrite all along. They threaten to show the footage to the shop owner, to the police, to Maz's parents, to the school.

> *I can't believe this is the same girl who has literally given me grief all year for the way I dress. She's been awful to me.*

Morgana laughs softly, shaking her head in disbelief. She doesn't know how it happened, but somehow, in a beautiful twist of events, Maz has been dealt with and she did it to herself. The timing couldn't be better.

> *Right? Last week she told me that she was taking some of her old stuff to the charity shop if I wanted to buy something fashionable for a change. Right in front of everyone – it was mortifying.*

She acts like she's untouchable – but I bet her parents are going to cut off that money supply pretty fast when they get an eyeful of this. LOL. She deserves everything that she gets. She's going to be frozen out of every group in Avalon for this. She's silenced now. Nobody will ever listen to her ever again.

Frozen out. Silenced…

Morgana swings her legs out of bed and dashes out of her room, racing down the sweeping staircase to the kitchen and then through the side door into the garage. She hadn't wanted to risk Art finding her spell so she put it in the big chest freezer that is rarely used, knowing it was unlikely to be disturbed out there. Now she opens the lid and rummages behind the loaves of bread and the housekeeper's uneaten casseroles, pulling out the jar and holding it up in front of her, tilting the glass from one side to the other.

The liquid inside is solid, Maz's face blurred inside the ice.

Slowly she closes the freezer and makes her way back to her room. She can hear Mabel/Mavis vacuuming somewhere in the house and Art's trainers are still by the front door, so it's safe to assume that he's still in bed. Nobody is going to disturb her, which is fortunate because her head is reeling with thoughts and she needs some space to think all this through.

Morgana carefully places the jar on top of her shrine and stands before it, breathing in deeply and sending her thanks out into the universe. Nobody is going to listen to anything Maz says ever again.

Morgana did this.

She froze Maz out and all she had to do was manifest it into being. That's why her throat is hurting – she has removed Maz's ability to be heard and the magick always demands a return on her part. Brigid was right when she said that someone always has to pay.

Walking across to her window, she stares at the black feather lying on the small balcony outside, almost certain it wasn't there when she opened the curtains earlier.

When a feather appears, the end is in sight.

Deep inside, the ever-present rage bubbles a little less than normal. She finds the knowledge of her power both soothing and scary. If she's ever had doubts about her powers – the same powers that sent Alice out on to the cliff path that stormy night – then those doubts are now gone.

She is not a victim.

She can do anything she wants to anyone she wants.

And she's only just getting started.

Protection Spell

You will need:

A seashell

I. Hold the shell in your hand and close your eyes.

II. Imagine a protective barrier forming around you, that moves with you as you walk.

III. State the following mantra:
<u>Protect and keep me safe from all harm.</u>

IV. Repeat the mantra three times.

V. Keep the shell on you as a protective amulet.

CHAPTER 14

Can we talk…?
Morgana…?
I haven't done anything wrong.
Please don't do this…
Look, I'm sorry, OK?
I know what you're doing.
Don't push me away, Morgana. I'm begging you…
You don't understand what it's been like for me…
Did you set this up? Is this because of the Lance thing…?
Was it you who filmed me?
Please text me back. You can't throw away four years of being Sisters…
Screw you, Morgana. I won't forget this…

Morgana needs some air. Satisfying as it is to have Maz reaping the karmic rewards of her actions, knowing that she's responsible for this mighty downturn in Maz's reputation is still a lot to process. She must be careful; she knows that. After what happened with Alice, she needs to harness her energy to exert just the right amount of penance to those who have wronged her. She needs to keep control, not lose her head.

She cast another spell this morning. It's just something daft, really – a bit of fun to practise channelling her powers. This time her target is Vivi.

She might feel just the tiniest bit sorry for Vivi these days, and she appreciates the other girl standing up for her with Maz and Ginny, but her near constant presence at Pendragon Hall has always irritated her and it seemed the perfect opportunity to have a go at another jar spell, although this one will be buried in the flower beds beside the front door instead of being put in the freezer.

At least she has the house to herself for a change. Art disappeared at first light with Vivi, off to collect Ginny and Lance before heading to a beach round the headland from Avalon in search of some decent waves and they'll be gone for most of the day. She has hours to herself and nobody to disturb her.

Once she's finished writing her journal entry, outlining exactly what fate she wishes to befall their neighbour, she pulls on her trainers, buries the spell jar in the flower bed, and goes to the kitchen where she grabs an apple from the heaving fruit bowl that the housekeeper has left on the table. Then, making sure that she has her key, she steps out into the sunshine.

She has no plan but heads towards the shops. Despite Pendragon Hall feeling remote, it only takes a few minutes to walk into town. Morgana walks slowly, enjoying the fact that the High Street is crammed with tourists and that she can be invisible amongst them. There's no risk of bumping into anyone she knows in any of the new age, magick stores – the locals don't go anywhere near them. She's just debating popping into her favourite crystal shop when she sees a flash of flame red.

Without thinking, she walks straight past the entrance and follows Celeste, who seems to be moving faster and faster ahead of her. Morgana dodges round prams with screeching babies and yappy dogs on leads, intent on keeping her in sight.

And then Celeste disappears. Morgana speeds up, racing past the shop selling bundles of herbs and the old man who will read your aura for twenty pounds, desperate to spot her. She reaches the end of the shops and spins round to see if she's somehow missed the other girl. The street stops at this point. The only options are that Celeste has gone inside a shop or has taken the track that leads towards the Tor.

Morgana hesitates for a second and then darts off the street and up the track.

The path banks steeply upwards and her pace slows

as she starts to tire. Halfway up, it splits into two, one to the Tor and the other to the forest. This is stupid. It's hot, she's got an exam tomorrow and she's racing around Avalon searching for a girl who she doesn't know and who never seems to stay in one place for longer than a couple of seconds. It's impulsive and Morgana doesn't do impulsive. She should turn round, go back down the hill, buy an ice cream from the amazing gelato parlour and head home.

Then a flash of red flickers in the treeline, as if the forest is on fire, and Morgana breaks into a run, led like a moth towards the flames.

She steps off the path at the point where she saw Celeste vanish and the rest of Avalon seems to fade into the distance. It's much cooler under the trees, the canopy stopping the sun's heat and light from getting through. Morgana's feet sink slightly into the ground and, when she looks down, she can see that her shiny white trainers are covered with the leaves, bark and twigs that litter the forest floor. Shivering, she walks forward, searching for any sign of Celeste and trying to ignore the sensation that the trees are pressing in on her.

Above, a bird makes a loud sound and then something scuttles in the bushes to her right, making her jump. Nobody ever hangs out here – the beach and the Tor are where all the action is. The forest has its own folklore. Brigid's voice rings in her ears.

Stay out of the forest, Morgana. The trees have a duality – they contain lightness and shadows; dreams and nightmares; truth and lies; friends and enemies. She'd fixed Morgana with a stern look, her face serious. *Until you understand your own strength and your own weakness, the forest is no place for you to stray. Not until you know your motivations. The trees will sense your power and they will want it for themselves, so stay away.*

But still she keeps walking away from the path, as if something is pulling her forward. Little Red Riding Hood at the start of the story – if she was going in search of a frustrating, beguiling girl and not taking cakes to her grandmother.

And then Morgana sees three things at once.

A break in the canopy, allowing a bright beam of sunlight to stream through the leaves like a spotlight, illuminating a clearing.

A huge tree, with colourful ribbons and other strange-looking items strung from its lower boughs, a mass of branches and twigs piled up to create a large circle round the outside.

Celeste, leaning against the tree and staring right at her.

And even though she's found what she was looking for, Morgana is overcome with the urge to turn on her heels and run for her life.

The bird caws again and Celeste raises a hand.

"Stay," she says, as if she can read Morgana's mind. "Just for a minute. I want to show you something."

It's witchery. It must be. Morgana reaches the branch circle and pauses, her eyes fixed on the girl in front of her.

There is a tension in the air that she can't quite place and she isn't sure if it's coming from her, Celeste or something else entirely.

"You can just step over it," Celeste tells her. "It's a protective circle and when you're in here you're perfectly safe."

Morgana looks down. She could leave now, walk away and pretend that this never happened. But if she steps over the circle, there's no going back. Morgana knows this as an absolute fact even as her feet lead her forward and towards whatever this is.

Celeste tilts her head to the side. "Can you hear that?"

"No." Morgana's heart is pounding in her chest as she steps into the circle and comes to a halt in front of the girl and the tree. "What am I supposed to be hearing?"

"Nothing." Celeste smiles and Morgana sees that out here, in the forest, her eyes are now the deepest moss green. "You aren't *supposed* to hear anything. I just wondered if you *could* hear it, that's all."

"You wondered if I could hear nothing?" Morgana scowls, feeling suddenly annoyed. She hasn't come all the way out here to be spoken to in riddles.

"Why *did* you come here?" asks Celeste, and Morgana takes a step back, again alarmed at the apparent mind-reading. She should leave. She doesn't know this girl and it suddenly dawns on her that she hasn't told anyone where she is. Celeste could hit her over the head with one of the branches that are lying on the ground and bury her body in a pile of leaves and nobody would ever be the wiser. She should have listened to Brigid's words of warning. But she didn't, and she is here now.

"Why are *you* here?" she demands, reminding herself that she is Morgana Merrick and that people fear her, not the other way round.

Celeste tips her head back, the green velvet choker dark against her neck.

"That's why," she says. "Look."

Morgana stares at her for a second and then tilts her own head backwards, looking up at the tree above her. The colourful ribbons that she saw as she entered the clearing flutter in a breeze that can't be felt on the ground. Sticks bent into the shape of stars and triangles dangle from strings, like mobiles above a baby's cot. Animal bones, wrapped with leather cord, are suspended from the branches.

And then a sound. Tiny, very faint, almost inaudible but definitely there.

The ringing of a bell.

"You hear it, don't you?" Celeste puts her hand on Morgana's arm and Morgana doesn't shake it off. "I know you can hear it."

"Where's it coming from?" Morgana scours the branches. She can see pine cones hanging from thread and twigs woven into strange shapes, but no bells.

"I don't know." Celeste steps to the side, moving towards the logs and branches that form the circle and Morgana feels a sudden sense of emptiness. "I've been looking for days and I can never see it."

"What is this place?" Morgana looks over at Celeste, who is now sitting on one of the upturned logs. "Why have I never heard about it?"

Celeste shrugs. "It's always been here – I guess you never wanted to find it before."

"Who are you?" She stares at the other girl, her red hair flowing around her shoulders and on to the spaghetti straps of the long green dress that she's wearing. With the sun beaming down upon her, she looks ethereal, otherworldly. "Where did you appear from?"

Celeste laughs gently. "I'm a forest witch and I've always been here. Maybe you never wanted to find *me* before, either."

Morgana makes her way to where she's sitting, perching beside her on the log so that they are both facing the tree.

"Are you always so annoying?"

"Yes."

"Good to know."

They sit in silence for a minute or so and then Morgana cracks.

"Come on then. You didn't answer my question. What is this place?"

Celeste peers at her quizzically. "Do you really not know?

Morgana shakes her head. "I've heard things about the forest being haunted but I've never heard anything about any weirdly decorated trees, no."

"But you did hear the bell?" Celeste suddenly looks worried, as if she's made a mistake and, for an awful moment, Morgana thinks that she's going to get up and leave.

"I heard the bell," she confirms, her words rushing to be heard.

"OK." Celeste leans forward, resting her elbows on her knees and stares up at the huge old tree. "Do you know anything about the stories of Avalon and the legends that it's built upon?"

Morgana nods. "Yes. But most of them are either to do with the sea cave or the Tor. I've heard some things about the forest – that it's unsafe for women and girls. But nothing about this tree."

"And you've never been in here before?"

Morgana opens her mouth to confirm, and then remembers. "Once. I came up here when I first moved to Avalon. I only got a few steps into the trees, though – nowhere near as deep in as we are now."

"Why didn't you go any further?" Celeste is looking at her with genuine interest.

"It felt … wrong," she says. "Dark and a bit scary. Like something was watching me. Kind of—" She stops, not wanting to make a complete fool of herself.

"Foreboding?" finishes Celeste.

Morgana laughs quietly. "Yes, which was completely ridiculous because right now it feels fine. Anyway, I never came back here again."

"Where *do* you go?" asks Celeste, and Morgana knows exactly what she means. *Where do you go to feel safe?*

"The sea," she answers. "I love the waves and the feeling of salt spray in the air. It's wild and fierce and out of control – and that makes me feel *in* control."

Celeste nods. "A sea witch. That makes sense."

Morgana leans down and picks up a leaf, letting it crumble under her fingers while she debates how to reply. Her power isn't something she's discussed with anyone since Brigid left, yet Celeste is dropping it casually into the conversation, as if it's no big deal.

Celeste smiles. "That's how I feel about the forest."

"Really?" Morgana frowns. "There's nothing wild and fierce about trees."

"Are you sure?" Celeste waves her hand around the clearing. "You don't think being amongst living things that have been here for hundreds of years and witnessed more than we ever can … is wild? I love the smell of the earth after a rain shower and the way you can taste the dampness on your tongue. But anyway, it's not about wild and fierce for me – it's about connection and solidity and feeling part of something bigger. Shall I tell you the story of this tree?"

She stands up, offering a hand to Morgana, who takes it unhesitatingly. Then the two girls walk forward until they're standing next to the trunk, one hand each on the rough bark.

"It was 1737 and Avalon was ravaged with smallpox," Celeste begins. "Many people died and the locals were scared. So they did what people always do when they don't understand why something is happening and looked for someone to blame. Luckily for them they had an easy scapegoat – the four Gretel sisters who lived nearby."

It seems to Morgana that she can't go anywhere without being confronted by *sisters* these days.

"Why were they blamed?" asks Morgana. "Did they bring the smallpox to Avalon?"

"No." Celeste shakes her head. "They had committed the double sin of being outsiders and women, and that was all it took for the townspeople to be convinced that they were the root of all evil."

"So what happened?"

"The townspeople accused the sisters of witchcraft and dragged them out to this spot." Celeste releases Morgana's hand and presses both of hers against the tree trunk. "They bludgeoned them to death and then buried them in four separate locations so that they couldn't conspire in death against the locals."

"That's horrible." Morgana shivers again, despite the shaft of bright sunlight.

"It was." Celeste's voice holds a tremor. "But then a beech tree mysteriously grew on each of the graves and they became known as the Witch Trees. The other three have all been destroyed in storms but this one remains – the tree that marks the grave of the youngest sister Silke. She was only sixteen years old when she was killed. Everything on here has been placed as a gift to the wronged Gretel sisters."

"Who puts them there?" Morgana stares up at the trunk, spotting a tiny doll-like figure nestled in one of the hollows. It's a poppet, a doll used in witchcraft, and it should be creepy but it isn't.

Celeste turns and leans her back against the tree. "I don't know. Other girls? I've never seen anyone up here but every time I come there's a new trinket or talisman."

A gust of air sweeps through the woods, the tiny sound of tinkling bells on the wind.

"Will you come here again?" asks Celeste, gazing at Morgana.

"Only with you," Morgana tells her. "And next time with an offering. Can I get your number?"

Celeste laughs quietly. "I don't have a phone."

Morgana blinks. "What do you mean? Who doesn't have a phone these days?"

'Me."

"So how am I supposed to get in contact with you?"

Celeste steps forward and turns to look back at the Witch Tree. "See that hole in the trunk? You can leave me a note in there if you want to see me."

Morgana huffs. "That's ridiculous. Are you serious?"

Celeste nods. "Deadly. And what you heard about the forest wasn't right, you know." She jumps over the circle and gestures for Morgana to join her. "It's not that it isn't safe for women and girls. It isn't safe *because* of the women and girls – there's a big difference."

The air between them fizzes and Morgana isn't sure

whether the bubbling up inside her is laughter or fear. What she is sure of is that whatever this is, it is bigger than her.

Slowly, not breaking eye contact with Celeste, she steps out of the protective circle and then together, without speaking, they walk back through the trees and towards the path, towards Avalon, towards something new.

You-Messed-with-the-Wrong-Witch Spell

You will need:

9 thorns from a blackthorn tree   An airtight jar

3 red baby chillies   1 teaspoon of chilli powder

I. Place the thorns and the chillies inside the jar, saying the following words:
  <u>The burn of the chilli,</u>
  <u>The bite of the thorn.</u>
  <u>The moon in the night,</u>
  <u>And the sun in the morn.</u>

II. Add the chilli powder, saying:
  <u>All through the night and every day</u>
  <u>You are not welcome so please stay away.</u>

III. Seal the jar and rotate it three times anticlockwise, saying:
  <u>From the sun's rise until it doth set</u>
  <u>Don't enter this place or you'll suffer regret.</u>

IV. Bury the jar close to your front door.

CHAPTER 15

"That exam was pure evil." Lettie flings herself dramatically forward, resting her head on her arms. "Whoever came up with those questions needs to be fired – no way was that GCSE level."

Iris pats her on the arm. "I'm sure you did fine," she tells her. "Everyone always thinks they've done badly after an exam."

"I mean, they were pretty textbook questions," says Morgana, reaching for her drink.

It's quiet at the Shack today with most people choosing to go home after school and revise for the next round of exams, but Lettie had demanded a gathering of the Sisters and, given their rapidly depleting numbers, it seemed prudent to keep her and Iris happy. That doesn't mean pandering to Lettie's stupidity, though.

"At least two of the twenty-mark questions were identical to ones that Mr Williams gave us for homework a few weeks ago," Morgana continues, hiding a smile when Lettie's head whips up to look at her in disbelief. "So I'm sure you got those right. Don't stress about it."

"I didn't do the homework!" Lettie's wail drifts across the sand towards the surfers. "I was too busy learning knitting for that hand-modelling gig for the crafting magazine. Oh god, this is a freaking nightmare!"

"At least you can whip up a nice cosy scarf for yourself now – it's not all doom and gloom, is it?" Morgana smiles kindly at Lettie, whose eyes have narrowed slightly as if she's starting to doubt Morgana's sincerity.

Took her long enough.

Morgana glances at her phone, noting with frustration that the battery is perilously low, and then downs the rest of her drink. "Anyway, I'm going to love you and leave you. We've got chemistry tomorrow and I'm in no way ready."

Giving them a cheery wave, she steps off the decking and walks up towards the road above the beach, heading into town. She's lying. Of course she's ready. Her revision has been carefully planned, just like everything else in her life. Today is about chemistry of another kind.

Celeste is waiting for her at the top of the track, just as Morgana requested in the note she left at the Witch Tree. Wordlessly they step into the woods and slip between the trees, Morgana already feeling familiar with the path that she can now see is trodden into the bracken and ferns, presumably trampled by the feet of the other people who make this pilgrimage. She still doesn't know anything about this girl, other than she makes Morgana's heart beat faster, which is undoubtedly caused by some kind of spell work on Celeste's part.

It's cooler today, the sky overcast and filled with ominous-looking clouds. Twigs crack underfoot as they push their way through the undergrowth.

"Damn!" Morgana stumbles as a particularly aggressive bramble makes a grab for her. "That hurt!"

"Let me see." Celeste crouches down to look at her bare leg, which is now dotted with tiny spots of blood. "Yeah, it looks kind of bad. You might need an ambulance."

"What?" yelps Morgana, before catching herself. "Oh shut up! It hurts, you witch. How about some sympathy? Stupid bramble."

"Sorry." Celeste stands up and grins at her. "But don't blame the plant. It's only defending itself – as far as it knew you were about to rob it of its fruit."

"What fruit?" Morgana rolls her eyes. "Blackberries don't even arrive until at least July."

Celeste laughs. "We'll make a forest witch of you yet. I've known many in my time and you definitely have something special."

Morgana opens her mouth and then closes it again. She has questions, so many questions, but none that need an answer immediately.

"Come on." Celeste pulls her by the hand. "I know where we can find something to help."

They continue through the woods and then the Witch Tree is there in front of them.

Celeste darts forward, stooping to pull something out of the ground before bounding back to Morgana, a large broad oval-shaped leaf in her hand.

"Rub your leg with this," she tells her.

"What is it?" Morgana doesn't move. "I'm not a little kid who can be fobbed off with some placebo-effect rubbish."

"It's called broadleaf plantain. Just try it." Celeste thrusts it at her and Morgana reluctantly accepts the leaf. "Are you always this stubborn?"

"Yes." Morgana leans forward and presses the leaf against her leg. The cooling effect instantly soothes the scratches.

"Good to know."

They smile at each other and Morgana feels a fizz of something deep within her. If she didn't know any better, she would say it was happiness.

"Where do you live?" she asks Celeste. "I've never seen you walking home from school, so I'm guessing you don't live on my side of town."

Celeste throws her arms out, as if she's embracing the forest. "I live here," she proclaims. "The trees are my home."

"And what about your family?" Morgana rolls her eyes. "Are they forest sprites and pixies?"

"No." Celeste spins in a circle, looking up at the sky

through the canopy. "Don't be ridiculous. They're witches, obviously."

"Obviously."

Celeste stops spinning and looks over at her with curiosity. "What did you bring? For the tree?"

Morgana shakes her head, suddenly unsure. "Nothing."

"I don't believe you." It's a statement, not a judgement.

"Fine." She reaches into the pocket of her skirt and pulls out a shell. "I brought this."

Celeste stretches out her hand and runs the tip of her finger against the ridged surface. "Why?"

Morgana shrugs. "I don't know."

"Yes, you do."

"What did *you* bring?"

Celeste puts her hand into her own pocket and when she opens it up there is a stone lying on her palm, a symbol painted on to the smooth top.

"It's a rune," she explains before Morgana can ask. "I like making them out of pebbles and stones."

"What does the symbol mean?" Morgana traces the outline of the shape.

"It's called Jera," says Celeste. "And it symbolizes celebrations, the end of misfortune and the start of new beginnings. It means that things are changing and it's why I'm here."

"It sounds like something that I need," murmurs Morgana. "I'm definitely on for a new beginning."

"This *is* for you." Celeste presses it into her hand. "I've made another one for the tree." She pulls another stone out of her hand and shows it Morgana. "This one is Sowilo. It represents the sun and it's the rune I most associate with Silke because her name means heavenly."

"That's the same meaning as yours." Morgana smiles, pleased with the symmetry. "My name means *born of the sea,* which is kind of cool, I guess."

"Our enemies are always nearby." Celeste's voice is low and quiet as she steps inside the circle of protection, the stone in her outstretched hand. "Sowilo reminds us to use goodness to defeat evil and to shine the sun's light on our own dark natures. We need to be ready and we need to be brave. The Gretel sisters had courage but they failed to grasp their enormous power until it was too late. They weren't prepared and they paid with their lives. Sowilo tells us to question the motives of ourselves and those around us, and not be afraid of taking control."

She steps up to the base of the trunk and stands silently for a moment before placing the stone on top of one of the exposed roots, whispering a few words that Morgana cannot hear. Morgana pauses, unsure about what she's supposed to be doing and Celeste, without turning her head, reaches out her hand.

"There aren't any rules," she says softly. "You can give to Silke and her sisters in any way you choose."

Glancing quickly around to check that nobody else is in the clearing, Morgana crosses the circle and walks over to stand next to Celeste.

"I don't have anything deep and meaningful to say." She pushes the shell into a crack in the truck, so that it's barely visible. "I just thought that as this is literally the one place in Avalon where you can't hear the waves, it might be nice to bring the sound of the sea to the forest."

"I like that." Celeste looks at her with eyes that today are the colour of apples. "I think the Gretel sisters will like it too."

"I hope so." Morgana stares up into the branches where the ribbons are flapping back and forth. "It's so unfair. I bet that they didn't even get to defend themselves or have their say. Those people just made up their minds about them."

"It isn't changing other people's minds that is hard. It's way trickier to change your own opinion of yourself."

Morgana leans against the tree trunk, feeling the rough bark against her school shirt. "True. I've always found it exceptionally easy to influence what others are thinking."

Celeste is silent for a moment and Morgana has the uneasy sensation that she has somehow said the wrong thing. And then the other girl spins round and starts walking away and she knows that once again, she's managed to disappoint.

Which is fine.

Let Celeste leave.

She's got more important things to do than traipse around Avalon doing witch stuff where people might see her – like getting home and doing witch stuff in private, deciding exactly what punishment she is going to dole out to Lance, now that Maz has been dealt with.

"Are you coming?" Celeste calls, once she's stepped out of the protective circle of branches.

Morgana breaks into a trot to catch her up. "Where are we going?"

"You'll see." Celeste grins at her. "Somewhere special."

They walk out of the woods and down the track to the fork. Morgana takes a step towards town but Celeste puts out a hand to stop her.

"Not that way," she says. "We're going up there."

She nods in the direction of the Tor and Morgana groans.

"No way." She shakes her head. "It's full of tourists."

"Not for long." Celeste gestures upwards. Now that they are out from the cover of the woods, Morgana can see that the clouds are gathering, ready for what looks like an epic storm. They skitter across the sky, growing darker and darker by the second and she can feel the wind picking up, the leaves in the trees behind her going from a whisper to a frantic rustle.

The pathway up to the Tor is steep and exposed. As they start to climb, people start appearing in the opposite direction. A trickle at first and then, as the first raindrops start to fall, a flood of walkers cascading down the hill, desperate to make it back to town before the heavens open.

"We're going to get soaked!" calls Morgana.

"Yes!" shouts back Celeste.

And they keep climbing.

By the time they reach the top, the Tor is empty. There

is a rumble in the distance and then a flash of light on the horizon and Morgana stops thinking about her wet feet and instead slowly rotates, taking in the sight before her. She's been up here before; of course she has. The Tor is one of the major features of Avalon, and she can see it from her bedroom window, looming above the town with its single high stone tower whose turrets sometimes seem to touch the clouds. She knows the stories about this place; people believe that the Tor guards one of the two entrances to the Otherworld, the land of the dead, with the sea cave holding the other.

The story has never felt as real as it does in this moment.

Together, they walk through the open archway of the tower and across to the edge of the Tor. Below them, Avalon spreads out like a patchwork quilt, streets and buildings stitched in between fields of yellow, green and brown.

Morgana looks over at Celeste. "What are we doing up here?"

"We're reclaiming ourselves," Celeste shouts, her voice vying to be heard over the rain. "Up here, where the universe can hear us and where we can share our innermost truths about who and what we are."

She closes her eyes and holds her arms out on either side, like she's about to take flight. "I am Celeste! I call back my power – I am enough!"

Beside her, Morgana stares at Celeste's beautiful upturned rain-soaked face. It's true. She is enough.

She turns back and closes her eyes, raising her hands high into the air.

"Morgana Merrick!" The words are whipped away the second they are released. "I am Morgana goddam Merrick!"

"And what are you?" Celeste is right there, whispering gently in Morgana's ear. "Tell the universe exactly what you are."

Morgana laughs, and it sounds like thunder. Where should she start?

She is revenge.

She is control.

She is fear.

What she will never be is enough, but maybe that's just something she's going to have to live with.

Morgana's hair flies around her face and the rain lashes at her. Celeste grabs her hand and squeezes it. Lightning flashes, nearer this time and something inside her is unlocked.

"I am Morgana Merrick," she roars, "and I am everything!"

Beside her, Celeste's hand tightens its grip.

"Universe, hear us," she shouts, "and let it be so!"

And then they're running back to shelter of the tower, huddled together out of the storm, breathless and laughing and holding on to each other as if their lives depend on it.

"What's that?" asks Morgana once they've got their breath back. She points at a strange shape scratched into the stone next to them.

"It's a sigil," she says. "A symbol. Chaos witches use them to make their magick work."

"Everything is chaos when I'm with you," Morgana tells her, feeling her heart beating double-time in her chest. "But what's a chaos witch specifically?"

Celeste frowns. "Chaos witches believe that anyone can do magick. That there aren't any specific rules. And they aren't bothered about whether magick is good or bad, which is interesting but … it can be dangerous."

"So what's with the sigil?"

"They're actually kind of brilliant." Celeste traces the outline with her finger. "You write down your intention, as though it's already happening – you know, something like *I am happy* or whatever you want to manifest, and then you take out all the vowels and repeating letters and what's left becomes the symbol."

"So what does this one say?" Morgana squints at the shape, trying to see letters.

"Nobody except the sigil writer knows. Which is exactly how it should be – it's their desire and we don't need to know about it."

"Boring," drones Morgana. "Where's the fun if it's a secret?"

Celeste raises an eyebrow at her. "Are you telling me that you don't think secrets can be fun?" She leans forward and briefly rests her forehead against Morgana's own and then darts off, back into the rain.

Morgana watches her for a second, dancing in the

storm and not caring about her soaking clothes or her dripping-wet hair that hangs in tendrils around her face, looking as if she might twirl off the top of the Tor and disappear in an instant. Her stomach flips at the thought of Celeste's absence and she runs to join her without a single thought of how they're going to get back down the now -treacherous, slippery, wind-swept hill, or what will be next.

All she knows is that she needs this girl like she has never needed anyone. Questions can come later.

CHAPTER 16

The walls of Pendragon Hall throb with music. The uneasy truce that existed between her and Art was destroyed the night they argued, and his friends have been an almost permanent fixture after school and into the evenings for most nights this week. And her hex against Vivi has clearly not worked – she's here all the time. Morgana grudgingly acknowledges that her hexing skills clearly need some work.

She flings her revision book down and howls a silent scream into her pillow. She could ask Art to turn the music down but she's seen him in this selfish, self-absorbed mood before and knows that there's little point in trying to reason with him. Plus, going downstairs would mean risking being in the vicinity of Lance and she's not up for that. Not while she's still debating which spell to use against him.

Sitting up, she looks across the room to her shrine, where the poppet that she made last night when she got home from the Tor sits, staring at her with its stitched eyes. She's no seamstress, but she's quite pleased with the results of her labours. It might not look particularly lifelike but it has two things in common with Lance – it's drenched in sandalwood oil and it's creepy. She wrote his name on a slip of paper and put that inside before she sewed it up, just for good measure.

The knock on her bedroom door is as surprising as it is unwelcome. Quickly she jumps up and drapes a silk scarf across the shrine, hiding it from prying eyes before returning to sit on her bed.

"Who is it?"

If it's Lance, then she's going to forget about hexing him and make do with hitting him over the head with her bedside lamp.

"It's only me." The door creaks open and Lettie's black braids hair swing into view. "I came over to see if you could lend me your revision notes. But Art says they're going in the pool – do you have a bikini I can borrow?"

Morgana stares at her. "Seriously? We've got an exam tomorrow. What about your revision?"

Lettie shrugs. "Let's get real – it's not going to make any difference now, is it? Anyway, I've got my modelling job at the weekend and if that goes well, then I won't need qualifications."

Morgana rolls her eyes, too bored to bother correcting her. Besides, it will be mildly entertaining to witness

Lettie's dawning realization that she's messed everything up once results day comes round.

"Why are you hiding up here, anyway? And don't give me any garbage about exams because we all know that you've been ready for weeks."

"I'm *trying* to relax—" starts Morgana, and then another head appears in the doorway.

"Morgana!" It's Ginny, with Vivi close behind her as always. "Come and join us. We need someone to make up the fourth for our game of pool volleyball because Lance can't come over tonight. Me and Art against you and Lettie – come on!"

"Get Vivi to do it," grumbles Morgana, her frustration rising. "Oh yeah, she can't go in water in case she melts. And what the hell is *that*?"

She points at Vivi, and the small white mouse on her palm.

"It's Geoffrey," Vivi tells her. "He won't bite."

"He's disgusting." Morgana shudders. "What is it with you and animals? You're like a wannabe Disney princess."

Vivi looks hurt. "What's wrong with liking animals?"

Morgana rolls her eyes at Lettie, who giggles. "Pleeeeaaase, Morgana? We haven't hung out in ages."

"I literally saw you two days ago," Morgana tells her. "Don't be needy."

"But you ran off early." Lettie pouts at her. "Iris and I are starting to wonder who it is that you're spending your time with."

Morgana groans internally. They aren't going to stop until she gives in and the last thing she wants is for them to start snooping around. Both Celeste and the magick are not something that she wants to share. Plus, she doesn't want people to suspect she's turning into a nerd.

"Fine." She gets up and walks across to her walk-in wardrobe, selecting her fourth-best bikini and throwing it across the room to Lettie. "I'll come down. But only because you asked so nicely."

Lettie whoops.

"Oh and, Vivi? Get that creature out of my room," Morgana snaps, eyeing the mouse. "Or I'll feed it to your cat."

Vivi retreats rapidly after Ginny and Morgana dispatches Lettie to the guest bathroom to get changed, while she quickly slips into her own bikini. Maybe this is exactly what she needs – to let off a little steam. She's ready for tomorrow – tonight can be about having some fun, which is a possibility without Lance's presence. For a brief second, she wonders what Celeste is doing right now and whether she'd come over to Pendragon Hall tomorrow to hang out if Morgana asked her, but then she rejects the thought. She isn't sure what she's got going on with Celeste, but, whatever it is, she wants it kept far away from Art and Lettie and the rest of them.

Downstairs, the game has already started. She pads through the kitchen and out into the orangery. The large pool dominates the far end, lit up with underwater lights and comfortable lounge chairs dotted round the side. Vivi reclines on one, Geoffrey now safely inside a small carry case. She flinches as someone splashes and Morgana snorts, thinking of the movie *Gremlins*.

"What happens if you get wet?" she calls. "Or eat after midnight?"

"What do you mean?" says Vivi, looking bewildered as usual.

Morgana sighs, already bored with the interaction. "Oh, never mind."

"Hurry up!" calls Lettie. "I'm losing over here."

Dropping her towel, Morgana walks round to the deep end and dives in, enjoying the instant silence as she hits the water. She makes her way towards the shallows where the others are standing, emerging next to Lettie and shaking the water from her hair.

"What's the score?" she asks.

"Three–one," shouts Art. "Get ready for it to be four–one in exactly two seconds."

He slams the ball across the net and Morgana launches herself forward to volley it back, grinning when it catches him on the chin. That'll teach him to hold a party the night before she has an exam.

"Go, girl!" yells Lettie in excitement, and then she looks anxiously across the pool at where Art is rubbing his face. "Are you OK, Art? *Oh là là!*"

"Give it a rest. He's fine." Morgana pushes herself backwards, ready to receive what will no doubt be a fierce pass. "Play on!"

Art passes the ball to Ginny, who manages to tap it

over the net before Lettie can reach it. Art roars in approval and grabs his girlfriend, whirling her around in the water while she squeals.

"Get a room," huffs Morgana. "God, you guys are insufferable."

"I think they're cute together," says Lettie, gazing at the couple with envy in her eyes.

"*So* cute," echoes Vivi from the lounger, and Morgana reminds herself that throwing up in the pool would be messy experience. "Does anyone want anything? I'm going to get another drink so I can bring some. Or a snack? Or…?"

"We're fine," barks Ginny. "Jeez, Vivi. Stop asking us every five minutes."

Morgana watches Vivi scurry off, feeling vague pity towards her. That was her in a previous lifetime – everyone's punch bag. If it wasn't for her magick, it might still be.

They continue to play for a bit longer and then the ball gets knocked out, rolling across the floor of the orangery until it comes to a stop at the feet of someone who has just walked in.

"You lost your balls, Art?" calls Lance, picking it up and holding it aloft like a prize.

"Dude!" Art grins at him. "I didn't think you could make it."

Lance is already stripping off his T-shirt . "Well, here I am."

Vivi appears behind him, a glass of juice in one hand and a bowl of crisps in the other.

"I brought snacks!" she calls. "I'm just going to go and grab some carrot sticks in case anyone wants a vegetable. But no worries if not – it's no bother."

Lance turns to smirk at her and she scuttles back to the kitchen.

Morgana watches as Ginny swims to the side of the pool and hoists herself out, the water dripping from her long hair making her look even more like a mermaid than usual. "You can take my spot," she tells Lance, smiling goofily up at him. "I'm happy to take a breather and watch you guys."

"I'd better give you all something to look at then, hadn't I?" Lance flexes his muscles and winks at Ginny – and Morgana wonders just how hard she'll have to throw the ball to be sure of doing some damage.

"Let's change teams!" trills Lettie. "I'll go with Art and Lance can go with Morgana."

"No," says Morgana, but it's too late and Lettie has already ducked under the net and is busy high-fiving Art. Morgana glares at her, trying to convey with her eyes that this is not acceptable, but Lettie's attention is on Art. Morgana realizes that she's been played. Lettie didn't care about hanging out with her – this was all a pathetic ploy to spend time with Art. She knows about the incident in the cave and how spending any time with Lance is the last thing that Morgana would want to do – and she doesn't care.

"Looks like it's me and you then, M." Lance enters the water and swims a few broad strokes across to where she is standing. "Again. This is becoming something of a habit."

He winks at her and something snaps.

"I'm out," she calls, not taking her steely gaze from his smirking face. "There's a bad smell over here."

"Aw, don't be like that, sweetheart." Lance reaches out and tucks the white Mallon streak behind Morgana's ear, and her fury bubbles over. She jerks her head back while simultaneously swinging her arm up towards Lance's face. He flinches, trying to block the blow and she stumbles straight into him, her arms thrashing wildly as she attempts to steady herself.

Across the net, Lettie and Art are splashing water at each other and shrieking, while Ginny looks on. Nobody is paying any attention to what is going on at the other end of the pool.

Lance rubs his head. "There's no need to get physical, M." He smirks at her. "Not like *that*, anyway."

Morgana glares at him and starts wading towards the steps. "In your dreams."

"You're always in my dreams." Lance is following her. "If you leave now, people will think you're a bad loser."

Morgana whirls round and takes a step towards him, her hands clenched at her sides. "The only person losing around here is you," she hisses. "You won't know how and you won't know when, but you're going to get yours, Lance."

"Is that a promise?" he calls, laughing as she hauls herself out of the water. "I can't wait."

"Me neither," she murmurs, grabbing her towel and wrapping it securely round herself. "Me bloody neither."

She stomps away, acutely aware of three things. The first is Lance's eyes boring into her as she leaves. The second is that nobody else, not even Lettie, her *Sister*, notices her go – and that is unforgivable. The third is that in her closed fist are several hairs, ripped from Lance's head as she flailed in the water. And much as she hates to have anything of him touching her, the hairs could be useful.

Back in her room, with the door safely locked and her pyjamas on, Morgana unpicks some of the stitching on the Lance poppet and pushes one of the hairs inside before storing the others in a glass jar as an insurance policy. Then she retrieves her Book of Shadows from the shrine on her chest of drawers. Her hands are shaking as she writes out a spell for Lettie, something to remind her that using Morgana is never, ever a good idea. Something to bring her bad luck.

Once she's done, Morgana leaves her room to gather the few ingredients that she needs from the kitchen, checking first that Vivi is back in the orangery. She's quiet, light on her feet and unnoticed by the group by the pool. The sound of their laughter fuels her fury and she moves fast, returning quickly to the sanctuary of her room. Casting the hex while Lettie is still in the house is sure to give it greater impact.

And then she sleeps. She sleeps and she dreams of water and roaring waves, engulfing Avalon and washing everything clean.

Spell to Bring Bad Luck

You will need:

1 teaspoon of salt

1 teaspoon of cumin

Opal tumbled stone

A pinch of ginger

A charm bag

I. Cast a protective circle using the salt.

II. Hold the opal in your hand and visualize the person who you wish to have bad luck.

III. Place the stone inside the charm bag.

IV. Add cumin to cast out good luck.

V. Add ginger to magnify the power of the spell.

VI. Tie the bag and put it on your windowsill (the spell will work better if there is a full moon).

VII. Leave it there until the magick is done.

CHAPTER 17

It's Friday. One more science exam to go before the half-term holiday and then a whole week off school. Morgana sits in the hall, trying to focus. All she has to do is get through the next ninety minutes and then she's free. She has plans for this week, and most of them revolve around spending time with Celeste. Their paths never seem to cross at school, but that's fine with Morgana; Celeste doesn't fit in at Avalon Academy – she belongs in the forest or on the Tor and Morgana has no desire to share her.

The paper is impossible. She can't understand it. She's revised non-stop for the last few months and aced every single mock test that they've been given, but today she can't catch a break. Every question has her doubting her answer and second-guessing her initial responses and each time she glances at the clock it seems to have sped up.

She finishes with only two minutes to spare, closing the paper thankfully. She can see Maz bent over her desk and frantically scribbling away. She's tried a few times to reach out to Morgana but she finally seems to have given up. Morgana sees her drifting around alone and looking like she's constantly on the verge of tears. Maybe she should have thought about that before she started spreading malicious rumours about people *asking for it*.

Across from Maz Lettie is leaning back in her chair, from the set of her shoulders seemingly relaxed. Perhaps a miracle has happened and she somehow managed to gain some knowledge between late last night and this morning. Or perhaps she's too stupid to understand that she's just failed yet another exam. It doesn't matter either way. The hex is set. It's only a matter of time before the bad luck will hit Lettie. Morgana smiles to herself, despite her anxiety about her own answers.

"Put your pens down, please," intones the adjudicator at the front of the hall. "Do not leave your seat until instructed to do so."

Morgana stretches out her spine and suppresses a yawn. The next week lies ahead, empty and delicious. She'll head to the Shack first to show her face and then she's meeting up with Celeste. They're planning on heading into the forest for a ritual – Morgana isn't sure what Celeste has in mind but she's ready.

At least, she thinks she is. While she isn't exactly new to the whole magick thing, Celeste seems to have a different vibe to Morgana, and she knows so much. Her passions lie in nature and working in conjunction with whatever energies she can tap into. Harmony. Morgana is less interested in harmony and more intent on harnessing the power around her. They've spoken lots over the last few days and found plenty of commonality between them – their belief in the vibrations of crystals, their use of herbs to give strength to a spell – but Morgana hasn't shared her hexing with Celeste.

Something tells her that she wouldn't approve.

The students are released from the hall slowly and Morgana joins the throng of kids waiting to go down the stairs and out into the freedom of the holidays. It's hot and busy and someone jabs her in the ribs with their rucksack, making her hiss under her breath.

"How did you get on?" asks Iris, pushing through the crowd to stand beside her. "I didn't think it was too bad."

"It was fine," lies Morgana. "What's the hold-up?"

"I wonder how Lettie did?" Iris looks around for the other girl. "She was seriously stressed out about it yesterday afternoon. I was really worried about her."

"Oh?" Morgana gives a confused frown. "She came over to party at mine last night. Didn't seem concerned about it then."

Iris's face falls. "I texted her last night and she told me she was going to bed early."

Morgana winces. "She must have changed her mind."

"No!" Iris shakes her head vehemently. "She just knew that I'd try to stop her partying the night before an exam. It's not like she's exactly acing her studies right now."

"It was a bit tricky," Morgana confesses. "I wanted to revise but she insisted on us hanging out with Art and the others."

Iris nods. "She's letting her obsession with Art get out of hand. All she talks about is him — I think the whole modelling thing is about getting him to notice her. And it's why—" She stops.

"Why *what*?"

The crowd in front of them moves slightly closer to the top of the stairs.

Beside her, Iris looks awkward. "I probably shouldn't say this," she starts.

"Oh, you definitely should. Out of friendship, yeah?" Morgana steps forward, pulling Iris with her.

"It's why she's so desperate to stay in the group." The words rush out. "Maz wanted her to come with her and ditch the Sisters, but Lettie says that hanging out with you is her only way of getting close to Art."

The rage swirls and billows, like the clouds above the Tor.

"And what about you?" They reach the top of the stairs and come to another halt. "Did you want to leave the *Sisters*?" The word choice is deliberate. Iris is one of the biggest offenders for using the cringe-worthy name.

"Are you only staying friends with me because of what I can offer you?"

"No!" Iris's eyes widen and glance up to the left, and Morgana can smell the lie. "Absolutely not. It's me and you for ever, Morgana. And Lettie, of course."

Morgana cricks her neck from side to side, aware of a deep tension travelling up her back and into her skull. The storm continues to build and she focuses all her attention on keeping it contained.

And then there's a scream.

The kids around them start yelling and pointing.

"Let me through!" Morgana calls, pushing her way through and down to where Lettie is lying on the floor, her bag and its contents strewn around her. Morgana kneels beside her, quickly pocketing one of the items. Lettie isn't moving and Morgana stares at her with an increasing sense of dread that drowns out the fury.

Iris gasps, following her. "What happened? Is she OK?"

"She just fell," says one of the boys. "Like, straight forward, head first down the stairs."

"Someone get a teacher!" yells someone else and then Mr Williams is there, crouching down next to Morgana and gently resting his hand on Lettie's head.

"Everyone move away," he calls. "Let's give her some space, please."

"Is she dead, sir?" shouts a voice, and Morgana feels her body start to shake.

"She's not dead," Mr Williams assures them, and then

Lettie opens her eyes, groaning loudly and Morgana sinks back on to her heels in relief.

"What happened?" Lettie mumbles. "Where am I?"

"She's got concussion, sir!" shouts the same helpful kid, as other staff appear and start ushering the rest of Year Eleven out of the hallway.

"It looks like you fell down the stairs." Mr Williams exhales. "I need you to stay there while we get a first-aider to check you out. Is there anywhere that hurts in particular?"

"My arm." She moans and when Morgana glances down, she can see that Lettie's left wrist is sticking out an unnatural angle. The sight of it makes her want to throw up.

"Girls, you need to come away now." Mrs Kline, the Year Eleven head of year, puts a hand on Morgana's shoulder. "Lettie is going to be fine – although I sincerely hope she's right-handed because it looks like that wrist could be broken."

"No!" Lettie suddenly sits up, grimacing in pain. "I've got my modelling job tomorrow. I'm fine, really."

"You're not fine," Mr Williams tells her sternly. "Your wrist is going to need looking at and you've had a nasty bump to the head. Your parents are going to need to come and collect you."

"Love you, Lettie," Iris says tearfully, as Mrs Kline encourages them out of the corridor. "I'll call you later."

"Me too," calls Morgana automatically, but she's not

really thinking about what she's saying. Instead, her head is reeling – and what she saw on the floor next to Lettie.

"Do you have any idea how she fell?" asks Mrs Kline, opening the door and herding them out into the sunshine.

"It was really busy on the stairs," says Iris, dabbing at her eyes. "She must have tripped. Oh god, and now she won't be able to model for the craft magazine because you need two hands to knit. What a nightmare!"

"Morgana?" The head of year turns to look at her. "Did you see what happened?"

Morgana shakes her head. "No. Like Iris said, it must have been a horrible accident."

She's lying. Her shaking fingers reach into her pocket and stroke the black feather that was lying on the ground next to Lettie.

When a feather appears the end is in sight.

This was no accident. This was karma. And it's the reason for Morgana's awful performance in the exam. She wished bad luck on to Lettie and had to pay back the magick with some bad luck of her own.

If you ask for what you want, then you'd better be prepared to get it.

Seems like Gordon was right about that.

CHAPTER 18

Morgana doesn't go to the Shack after school. Everyone else dashes off, clearly keen to get to the beach and talk non-stop about the dramatic end to the exam. Iris is in their midst, teary and shaken, although Morgana strongly suspects that she's loving the attention.

Instead, she heads straight for the forest. She isn't meeting Celeste until later, but she has a question to ask and she needs to be alone.

Leaving the path, she pushes her way through the ferns, stepping over brambles and dodging their thorny grasp with ease now, her eyes dead ahead, searching for the first sign of the Witch Tree. Crossing the protective circle, she takes the black feather that she found out of her pocket and holds it up in the beam of sun that streams through the leaves. The distinct blue black shimmers in the light. It is the feather of a raven.

Sinking down to the ground, Morgana stares up at the tree, still holding the feather aloft in her hand. "Was this you?" she asks. "Are these feathers a sign from the Gretel sisters?"

The leaves rustle and, in the bushes, something stirs. Morgana whips her head round, feeling the prickling sensation of being watched, but there's nobody there.

There's only her – and she has her answer.

"It's me," she whispers. "*I* did this – with your help."

Standing, she steps forward and tucks the feather into a hole in the truck, where it quivers and trembles like her voice as she whispers to the tree. "Gretel sisters, accept this gift."

Then slowly, every sinew and muscle in her body taut like a violin string, she lies down in a shaft of light, letting her body sink into the forest floor until it feels like she's floating on air instead of lying on the hard ground.

She wanted Lettie punished, but not hurt – not like that. She shivers, despite the warmth, remembering the sight of her Sister lying on the ground. She could have died and it would have been Morgana's fault.

Like Alice.

Once could be excused as a mistake but twice is a decision.

The sky is a deep azure blue that reminds her of Celeste's eyes. She stares upwards, gazing through the gap in the forest canopy that acts like her own personal window on the universe. She hadn't realized before how the trees around the Witch Tree grow in a circle of their own; a protection beyond that which has been created by women and girls on the ground, using branches and logs and twigs. Above her, clouds scutter across the sky and she lets her mind rise to join them before going further – up, up, up.

Through the troposphere, with its clouds and planes.

Then, the stratosphere, passing through the ozone layer as the temperature increases.

Next the mesosphere, dancing around meteors as they plummet down at speed, colder now.

Past the thermosphere.

Straight up through the exosphere, dodging the Earth's satellites with ease and taking a moment to wonder at the aurora borealis.

And then into outer space, where her thoughts crystallise and take shape before her.

She is both the ground she lies on and the atmosphere where her mind roams. She is dirt and she is air. She is dark and she is light. She is everything and she is nothing.

There is nothing that she cannot do.

She just has to harness it more effectively – not let the magick take control.

"It's beautiful, isn't it?"

Morgana is not sure when Celeste joined her because she has no idea how long she's been here. Twisting her neck, she sees the other girl lying beside her in the clearing and for a brief awful moment thinks that there is blood flowing out from her head, as if she's been bludgeoned. She blinks and sees that it's just Celeste's red hair, fanning out around her on the ground.

Morgana swallows the image away. "I don't think it's beautiful," she whispers. "I think it's powerful. I think you're beautiful, though."

Celeste turns her own head to look at Morgana, and they are now only centimetres apart.

"I think you're powerful," Celeste tells her, eyes sparkling with silver flecks of light.

Morgana reaches out her hand to take hold of Celeste's, their eyes, containing whole worlds and galaxies, locked on each other. Neither of them moves, but still they are pulled together like magnets and Morgana can smell the sweet scent of apples as she feels Celeste's soft, gentle lips on her own.

And as she swoops back through the atmosphere, diving back down to the forest floor, she knows three things.

One: she is invincible.

Two: there is no way that she deserves something this good.

Three: what happened with Lance was nothing like this. This will for ever be her first kiss.

Later, what could be seconds or years, Morgana neither knows nor cares, they stand, brush the dirt from each other and walk over to the Witch Tree.

"Who are you?" Morgana asks. "Honestly this time. Where have you come from? Where do you live?"

"Why does it matter?" asks Celeste. "I'm here with you right now. That's all that we have to think about."

Morgana stops beside the tree. "But how do I know that I can trust you? You know" – she puts her hand to her heart – "with this."

Celeste shrugs. "How do any of us know that we can trust anyone?"

"That's not exactly reassuring." Morgana scowls, and Celeste grins at her.

"Is that how you want me to make you feel?" she asks. "Reassured?"

Morgana shakes her head. "No. Yes. God, I don't know."

"Don't overthink it," Celeste tells her. "Now, do you want to cast a spell with me?"

Morgana nods, settling herself on to a root and leaning her back against the gnarly trunk while Celeste sits down opposite.

"What are we invoking?" Morgana asks her. "Something weird?"

She glances up at the raven feather, tempted to share the discovery of her increased powers with Celeste. Maybe she should tell her about the Lance poppet. She might even have some good ideas for how to bring him down.

But Celeste looks at her, a slight frown on her usually placid features. "I'm not invoking anything. I don't mess about with cursing spells or hexes – that kind of thing is usually connected to vengeance and harm. There's always a karmic price to pay for doing magick, good or bad, you know? And the payment for hexing can equal the damage done by the hex itself."

Morgana nods. She knows. It took three days for her sore throat to go away and no doubt she's going to be suffering for Lettie's downfall once results day comes round.

"The magick I'm interested in is about channelling what's around us and helping us tap into what we already have," continues Celeste. "To bring about good things."

"Sounds perfect." Morgana was right not to mention anything about the hexing. They have different opinions about magick, that's all. It's not a big deal.

"So this is a spell to invite love into your life." Celeste glances at Morgana anxiously. "If that's what you want? I mean, I don't really know what *this* is right now."

"I don't know either." Morgana swallows, feeling nervous. "But I do know it's what I want."

They smile at each other, both suddenly shy.

"OK." Celeste pulls two apples out of her bag, followed by a penknife. Morgana watches as she deftly cuts each apple in half horizontally, revealing the five-pointed star at its core. "I'm going to carve my initial into one half of the apple and the initial of the person I want to invite into my life on the other." Turning her back on Morgana, she inscribes something into the apple and then swivels back round, both halves of the apple placed together. She hands the penknife to Morgana. "You do the same."

Morgana doesn't turn away. Carefully, taking her time, she carves an "M" into the first half and then a "C" into the second before placing them on the ground between them. Celeste smiles, turning her own halves to reveal a "C" and an "M".

"That could have been awkward," says Morgana, and Celeste laughs. "What do we do now?"

"We bury them at the base of the tree," Celeste tells her. "And we ask the three Gretel sisters to open our hearts and our minds to each other."

"The four Gretel sisters," corrects Morgana. "And assuming that I'm your 'M'." She tries to make her voice light but a sliver of panic slides out with her words.

"You are most definitely my 'M'." Celeste picks up her apple and stands, the sun lighting her red hair from behind and making her look like a fire sprite. "Let's bury them together."

Morgana joins her, trying not to look at the raven feather, which is less than a metre from where they are standing, still shimmering like oil on water.

If Celeste has noticed it, then she hasn't said anything.

It's probably for the best.

CHAPTER 19

"Dad's home."

Art is waiting for her on the front lawn, his face screwed up in an unusual scowl.

Morgana sits down next to him and follows his stare, smiling when she sees the raven sitting on top of the stone porch above the front door

"And what joyous words of greeting did our loving father bestow upon you after being away for several weeks?" she asks.

"He asked me how I'd managed to spend so much money on garage invoices for my car and why the electricity bill is twice the usual amount." Art rips a daisy out of the grass and starts pulling the petals out one by one.

He loves me.

He loves me not.

Morgana shrugs, unsurprised that the first words out of Gordon's mouth were linked to finances. Anyway, Iggy has spent more time in the garage than she has on their driveway over the last few weeks. She isn't sure at what point Art will realize that the clapped-out old Jaguar isn't worth his efforts (or their father's credit card) but the car definitely has a limited life expectancy, whether he's prepared to admit it or not.

"Did you tell him that your many pool parties are responsible for the atrocious electricity usage?" she asks.

"No." Art tears his eyes away from the front door and looks at her. "But I didn't tell him that you spent most of the cash he left us at the local salon either."

Morgana raises an eyebrow, which only yesterday was plucked to perfection at that very establishment. "Fair enough. So I'm guessing that now isn't the right time to ask Gordon to buy me a new phone? The battery on mine is wrecked."

"Not unless you want to endure a lecture about what it was like growing up in the nineteen eighties when apparently the only technology in existence was a calculator, and he didn't even have one of those."

They grin at each other and then the sound of the door opening wipes the smirks from their faces.

"Morgana."

"Gordon."

Their father fills the doorway and Morgana thinks, not for the first time, how perfect Pendragon Hall is for him. Imposing, large, dominating – and with no soul or warmth.

"Exams?"

"Fine."

She learnt a long time ago that Gordon treats everything as a commodity, including words. He hands them out as if each one is costing him something; every communication is an interaction where he must come out in credit or, at the very least, not in debt.

"Excellent."

He jerks his head sharply, a sign of approval. "And how have you both been? I trust that Mabel has kept everything running smoothly?"

Morgana shrugs and, beside her, Art remains silent.

The seconds tick by and she resists the urge to giggle as Gordon's eyes start to narrow.

"There are a number of take-away meals on the credit card statement."

Art is the first to cave. "Mabel's food is the worst," he says imploringly. "It's not the same when you're gone – she makes an effort when you're around."

Gordon's mouth twitches. "Then it's just as well that I'm back."

Art grins and Morgana watches as he springs off the grass and approaches their father, who clasps his arms tightly and mutters something that she can't hear. It's different between them, she gets that – but it doesn't stop her enjoying the rare moments of snatched solidarity that she has with Art, or feeling the burn of once again being separate.

"How long are you staying this time?" she calls out when the heat gets too much.

Gordon releases Art's arms and starts down the steps towards his daughter, who stands up to meet him. "A few weeks at least," he tells her. "But don't worry, I'm going to be mostly in my study or out at conferences. I won't cramp your style – not when it's cost you so much already!"

Morgana smiles tightly. It's his idea of a joke, but the joke is on him, and not just his wallet. He's paid a terrible price for her being here – the loss of Alice is a cost far beyond pounds or dollars. The havoc she has wreaked on his life cannot be undone.

"It's good to see you, Morgana." He pulls her into a hug that feels as forced as his words.

"It's good to see you too, Gordon." He's trying to be a father to her; she knows that. But she's as much of a stranger to him as he is to her, even after four long years. A shared DNA can't ever make up for the lost time. Blood really isn't thicker than water.

"Are either of you in need of supper tonight?" Gordon asks as he pulls away.

"No!" They speak simultaneously, and then both laugh, trying to cover up the awkwardness.

"I'm hanging out with a few friends," says Art.

"And I'm seeing the girls for a chilled evening before

the next lot of exams start," adds Morgana. "We're just going to relax and have some fun."

"Sounds great," says Gordon, already halfway through the front door. "I'm not here either so I'll leave a note for Mabel."

Then he's gone, sucked into his study like it's a black hole and Morgana knows that they're unlikely to lay eyes on him for another few days.

"*Chilled evening*? Really?" says Art.

"Like you're just *hanging out with a few friends*," says Morgana. "I know what tonight is. It's a full moon in May – we both know what that means. Excalibur." Morgana fluffs her hair with her fingers. "Interesting that you didn't share *that* little piece of information with our father."

"Yeah, right." Art rolls his eyes. "I wasn't sure if you were going to grace us with your presence. You've missed the last few parties."

"I've been busy." Morgana pushes past him and through the door. "But I wouldn't miss *Excalibur*. Not for all the world."

Smiling sweetly, she glides up the stairs. Once in her room, she throws her bag into the corner, frowning when she sees the Lance poppet lying on the carpet.

"Trying to escape, are you?" she asks, picking it up and inhaling deeply, letting the scent of sandalwood and vanilla fill her lungs. "Good luck with that."

She'd realized this morning that tonight's activities offered the perfect opportunity for casting her humiliation hex on Lance. The spell bag is made – a small cloth bag filled with the relevant herbs and a crystal – and now she picks it up along with the poppet. She draws a circle with salt and places the bag and the poppet in the middle, saying the words that will make Lance feel all the pain and hurt that he has caused her, paid back twenty-fold.

Because she's generous like that.

CHAPTER 20

It's dusk by the time Morgana, Iris and Lettie step on to the sand below the Surf Shack. To the unobservant onlooker the beach is empty aside from a couple of dog walkers. The area where the kids from Avalon Academy usually congregate is quiet, but that's not where they're headed. Not tonight. Instead, they turn right and walk towards the headland that juts out into the sea.

"My arm hurts," whines Lettie after a few minutes. "Can we sit down for a moment?"

"No." Morgana keeps walking. "We're already late and there's no point in going at all if we aren't there at the start."

"Maybe you shouldn't have come?" says Iris, looking at Lettie with concern. "I'd walk you home but then Morgana will be all on her own out here."

"I'm not going home!" says Lettie.

"I'm fine on my own!" snaps Morgana at the same time.

"Fine." Iris holds her hands up. "I was just making a suggestion. Your arm sounds painful, Lettie."

"It really is." Lettie grimaces, struggling to keep up with Morgana's fast pace. "But even worse is the pain of discovering that the fashion world denies opportunities to anyone who isn't one hundred per cent perfect."

"Well, there's a massive surprise," drawls Morgana, picking up yet more speed. She can see people further ahead, making their way round the headland on the tiny footpath that is more suitable for sheep than people. They can't be late for *Excalibur* – she'll abandon Lettie here if she must, sisterhood be damned.

"So did you ask the agency if they'd consider still using you as a hand model, even with your broken wrist?" asks Iris.

"Yes!" Lettie's voice is indignant. "And they said no. Can you believe that?"

"Let me get this right," says Morgana, clambering on to the rocks that mark the start of the path. "Wasn't the photo shoot supposed to be of you knitting or something?"

"Yes, and I worked really hard to perfect my knit-one-purl-one technique."

Iris leans down and uses Lettie's good hand to help haul her up to the path. "It does seem unfair. Especially after you spent all that time learning how to knit in the first place. I bet you wish you'd done some revision now, huh?"

Lettie splutters a response and Morgana smiles in the growing gloom. She knew that Iris was too good to be true. Maybe there's hope for her yet.

They round the headland and Avalon disappears behind them. Ahead is a sight that looks like it's been ripped straight from a teen movie. A huge bonfire burns on the sand, surrounded by thirty, forty, fifty kids. Someone has brought drums and the rhythmic beating floats up to the path, giving the scene a vaguely macabre feel, as if someone is about to be sacrificed.

Which, if Morgana has anything to do with what happens tonight, is exactly what is going to happen. Metaphorically speaking, obviously.

The girls pick their way down the path and on to the beach. Morgana crouches down and removes her trainers, leaving them safely on the rocks for when she returns.

"I'm going to go and look for Art," she tells the others. "I'll catch up with you in a bit, yeah?"

Lettie ignores her, cradling her arm against her body.

Iris nods. "We'll just sit here for a few minutes," she says. "I think Lettie needs a rest."

They settle down on to the rocks and Morgana walks away. She isn't really going to find Art. What she's actually going to do is put the finishing touches to her spell and she can't do that with anyone around.

She heads along the side of the cliffs towards the sea, stopping once she's rounded a massive boulder that blocks her from view. The falling dusk provides a curtain of privacy but still she moves quickly, aware that anyone could appear and ruin the entire thing. Crouching down at the side of a small rock pool, she pulls the poppet out of her pocket and holds it up to her face.

> You think you are the best.
> You think you are so strong.
> But I am on a quest
> To show you that you're wrong.
> May you get what you deserve,
> May you show that you're a fool.
> Let your flaws and lack of nerve
> Be exposed to the whole school.

She had spent a while coming up with the perfect wording – Lance's fate needs to proportionate and fair and, after what happened to Lettie, she doesn't want to suggest anything too dramatic to the universe. A nice big dose of humiliation will work perfectly.

Carefully, gently she puts the poppet face down in the water, watching it float for a few seconds before the tiny stones that she filled it with drag it down to the bottom of the pool, just likes she wants to drag down his reputation. Morgana gazes at it, focused on channelling retribution to Lance and trying to ignore the prickle of unease that skitters in her stomach as Celeste's words about karmic payback flit through her mind.

Lance deserves whatever he gets. Besides, it's out of

her hands now. All she needs to do is sit back and enjoy the show. A smile breaks out across her face.

"Morgana."

Her smile vanishes. That voice is both unexpected and unwelcome. Glancing at the outline of the poppet under the water, she turns round to face Maz, who is dressed immaculately as usual, although her face is strained.

"What do *you* want?"

She has no idea how much Maz has witnessed but it seems sensible to come out on the attack.

"I want to talk to you," Maz says. "There are some things that I need to say."

"I don't think so." Morgana runs her fingers through her hair and steps forward, letting her shoulder knock into the other girl as she passes her. "Goodbye now."

"You can't keep on ignoring me!" Maz's voice rises in pitch.

"I can." Morgana doesn't look back at her. "And I will."

"But you can't ignore two of us." A figure steps out of the shadows. "Or do you think you're so powerful that you can take us both?"

Morgana pauses as Ro blocks her path. She's barely seen the other girl since she was removed from the Sisters and hasn't given her much thought at all. But here she is and, if Morgana isn't mistaken, issuing her with a threat.

Which just goes to show that neither Ro nor Maz have learnt a single thing from crossing her previously.

"What are you going to do?" she asks, tilting her head to the side in curiosity. "Out of interest."

"We want you to admit what you did." Maz edges past to stand beside Ro. "You set out to ruin us and we want to know why."

Morgana pouts. "That's not a very nice thing to say. You've hurt my feelings."

"You haven't got any feelings," snaps Ro. "Come off it, Morgana. You told everyone about me hooking up with Jayce and you posted that video of Maz on Avalon Asks. And we want to know why."

Morgana shakes her head. "It wasn't me who kissed the boy that my so-called *Sister* was pining after. And it also wasn't me that shoplifted a dress, despite constantly going on about how wealthy my family are. Probably because I am neither disloyal to my friends or a thief."

"So you don't think shaming us makes you disloyal?" Maz looks like she's about to cry. "You have everything, Morgana. It isn't exactly easy for the rest of us to live up to your expectations, you know."

"Interesting." Morgana stares at her. "So are you telling me that you're actually … poor? You were, what, stealing to keep up appearances?"

Maz winces, and even in the darkening light Morgana can see the embarrassment in her eyes.

"No." Her voice is quiet. "I don't know why I do it. Why I *did* it, I mean. But my parents are getting me some help."

"Perfect!" Morgana claps her hands and the sound

bounces off the cliffs. "So you're actually a poor little *rich* girl with issues." She smiles even wider and then lets the grin slide right off her face. "And this is my fault *how*?"

"If you really cared about our friendship, then you'd have spoken to us about what you knew." Ro shakes her head. "Not publicly humiliated us both."

"Not that it matters, but it wasn't actually me who posted that video." Morgana stares her down. "Still. Whoever it was did me a favour."

"You don't have to be such a cow," Maz snarls.

"No," agrees Morgana. "But it's a fun way to pass the time. Now, as much as I've enjoyed hearing your pitiful excuses, I need to go."

She struts forward, forcing them to step aside to let her pass in between them.

"You need to stop treating people like they're your puppets." Ro's voice is filled with warning and for a brief second Morgana feels a chill run down her spine. "You're going to have to pay, Morgana. Nobody can get away with behaving the way you do without consequence."

She considers them. "Is that a threat?"

"No." Maz narrows her eyes. "It's a promise."

"OK then." Morgana nods. She looks them up and down and smiles. Pathetic to think they can harm her in any way. "In that case I'll look forward to seeing what you've got in store."

Ro stares back at her. "We didn't say that it was us who are going to make you pay."

On the cliffs above a raven beats its wings.

CHAPTER 21

Over by the sheep path, Lettie and Iris are still waiting for her.

"Come on," Morgana tells them. "Things are about to get interesting."

"I'm not sure that I can…" starts Lettie, and then she looks at Morgana's face and gets to her feet. They walk over to the large group of kids gathering on the beach.

Anticipation hovers in the night air.

"They're about to start," yells a kid and the crowd surges forward, pulling Morgana, Lettie and Iris with them, down to the water's edge where the waves are crashing on to the sand, before dragging themselves back out with a sound that reminds Morgana of broken glass.

And there it is. *Excalibur.* The tall free-standing sea

stack just off the coast, rising out of the water like a sword, tall and thin and as deadly as its namesake.

Nobody knows how it first started, but every year, on the May full moon, the kids of Avalon flock to this part of the beach to watch the bravest, most foolhardy of them all jump from the stack.

"Look!" calls someone, pointing towards the steep rock face. "Art is going first."

Excellent. That gives her time to harness her power. Stepping forward, Morgana lets the water lap over her feet, the cold making her shiver for a second before her skin acclimatises to the temperature. Art is climbing Excalibur. The crowd is silent as he steps on to the ledge that forms the platform for this legendary but banned activity.

He doesn't even pause, instead launching himself off the edge without hesitation, his body seeming to soar upwards before curving down into a perfect swallow dive, his arms out to the side like he's flying – until he's about to hit the water, when he brings them forward, entering the sea like an arrow.

The crowd cheers, and now, of course, it's Lance's turn. Swiftly he scrambles up the rock to the same ledge, but unlike Art he doesn't jump immediately. Instead, he performs for the people, flexing his muscles and throwing a variety of over-the-top poses that make Morgana cringe and the girls around her seemingly weak at the knees. He's putting on a show, but Art's throwaway comment about Lance's fear of heights tells another story.

He's stalling.

Morgana takes another step forward, wanting to feel the cold against her ankles. She wiggles her toes and focuses on the sand that scratches the soles of her feet, blocking out everything around her except the feel of the water and the image in her mind of the poppet sinking to the bottom of the rock pool.

She's taken her time. She wanted to make sure that when she finally went after Lance that it would work; there's no room for mistakes.

And she can tell she is stronger. She can feel it. She has come so far in only the last few days. Celeste has helped too, not that she knows it. The more time that Morgana spends in her presence, the more useful her rage. Not that it's diminished or gone, absolutely not that. More that it has funnelled itself into something that can be channelled. Her magick is precise now, a laser point instead of a scatter gun. It is something that she can summon at will, which she can bend to do her bidding.

And what she is bidding it to do right now is to utterly humiliate the boy who has just stepped off a cliff. To drown him in mortification and embarrassment and disgrace.

There's a splash and a cheer and then he's there, hauling himself back on to the rocks and turning to wave to the crowd on the beach.

Morgana grins. The stage is set. The actors are assembled.

Lights, camera, witch, smile.

"He's so hot," a nearby girl mutters to her friend. "Sign me up for some of that, please."

"*So* hot," agrees Morgana, not turning round. "And wild too. I bet he'd tombstone off the top if everyone asked him to."

She closes her eyes, shutting her mind to everything except the thought of Lance spectacularly failing in full view of the entire student population. Her fingers reach up to grasp the obsidian necklace round her neck, an insurance policy to keep negative energies far away from her, and she imagines Lance making a complete fool of himself, humiliation that he can never live down.

And then, around her, the voices begin.

"Tombstone."

It's a murmur at first, almost a whisper.

"Tombstone."

Then louder, rippling out amongst the kids that line the water's edge.

"Tombstone, tombstone, tombstone!"

"Tombstone from the top!"

It's a chant, and the boy with the drums takes up the beat as feet kick at the water in time to the rhythm. Morgana opens her eyes to see the wind catching their words and whipping them across the waves and into the ears of the two boys who are standing at the base of the sea stack, preparing to jump in and swim back to shore.

"Tombstone from the top!" It's a howl.

"Tombstone from the top!" It's a demand.

Art looks up and flicks his hand dismissively before diving into the choppy waves and starting to swim back towards the beach. Morgana smiles again, this time with a feeling of relief. She knew that Art wouldn't give in to the pressure; that's not who he is.

Unlike Lance, who is now waving at the onlookers and bowing dramatically.

Your wish is my command. That's what Lance said.

Telling her that was his greatest mistake.

And so, as predicted, Lance starts to climb. She senses his hesitation as he passes the the original ledge, and seemingly the crowd does too because the chanting and drumming reach new levels.

"Tombstone!" It's a roar.

Morgana's fingers reach inside her pocket and she feels the fine mesh of the hex bag that she made earlier. It contains a cinnamon stick that she hopes will offer her extra protection against the bad karma she's invoking and some ground-up mugwort to amplify the magick, as well as a small piece of paper and a few rose petals – the May full moon is the Flower Moon and if she ever needed to harness the power of nature, then it is now. Yes, Celeste's teachings have been very helpful indeed.

Lance is almost at the top. He won't be able to do it. Nobody has ever jumped from Excalibur's peak before because nobody has ever been stupid enough to even contemplate it. The crowd presses forward and Morgana takes the opportunity to slip between the people who are craning their necks to catch every moment, gliding smoothly through the mass of bodies until she emerges on the other side and on to the now empty beach.

Heading up the sand, she walks round the bonfire to where she's unlikely to be spotted. Not that it matters if she is seen – she has a cover story in place. This was too stressful for her to watch after what happened to Alice.

An image of Art's mother flashes into her mind. Morgana wanted her gone. And then she was. Now she's using her powers on Lance. She's not twelve years old any more; she should know what she's capable of.

But he hurt her.

Come on. One little kiss.

He's not a good person.

And she does know what she's capable of.

Moving quickly, she pulls the piece of paper with Lance's name written on it out of the hex bag and holds it up to the flickering light. It's time for the second part of the hex to be carried out.

"By fire's light, I will make you pay tonight."

The words are quiet, barely audible in the night air, but inside her head they are loud screams of fury.

Rose petals flutter on to the flames.

She wants him to feel as awful as he made her feel.

The paper scrunches up inside her fist.

She wants him to be sorry.

"Feel the pain of humiliation's bite."

She throws the paper into the fire, watching the flames

consume the words. There is absolutely no way that Lance will jump from the top of Excalibur. He will have to scramble back down, revealing his fear of heights in front of everyone – and Morgana intends to make sure that nobody is left in any doubt about what a fake he really is.

Unless…

Unless that isn't all that happens.

Suddenly terror grips her. She sees Lettie's still body at the bottom of the stairs, remembers the shock she felt, and then the image is replaced with that of Lance floating lifelessly in the water. *No, not that…* Morgana shakes herself and gulps.

And then the chanting turns into a roar as Lance flies off the rock.

What has she done?

And what price is she going to have to pay for using her magick for such a terrible thing?

The beach hangs in suspense for a long second, a deathly silence crashing over the sand where everyone stands, staring out at the dark water. Then a collective gasp and the world starts turning again.

"Amazing!"

"Legend!"

The shouts hurl themselves towards her.

"He did it!"

The drumming starts up again, this time less sacrificial and more celebratory and suddenly kids are surging round the bonfire, whooping and cheering in delight.

The hex failed. She misjudged just how far Lance is

prepared to go. Morgana stuffs the hex bag back into her pocket and feels the heat of the flames on her face as, all around, people relive the magnificent, the daring, the legendary jump that Lance has just achieved. She's unable to tell whether she's annoyed or relieved that Lance didn't fail, but thinks it's probably a bit of both.

"And here's the man himself!"

Art appears across the fire, his arm draped round a dripping-wet Lance.

"I can't believe you did that, man," he tells him.

"I can't believe you didn't," Lance replies, his voice deliberately loud. "Guess you're just not that brave." He stares across the bonfire at Morgana, his face impassive as the flames flicker between them and, for a moment, it seems to her that he is not just a regular boy but something bigger, darker, meaner.

"It wasn't brave – it was dangerous and stupid, you loser." Art wrestles Lance to the sand and they tumble around while everyone laughs. Morgana is clearly the only one to have spotted the look of anger that flashed through Art's eyes. She wonders briefly whether things would be different if she'd told him what Lance did in the sea cave. Whether Art would have listened to her after all.

Iris appears beside her, Lettie hanging from her arm. "We need to go home. This is all too much for her – I knew she shouldn't have come out."

"You go on," Morgana tells her. "I'm going to hang out here for a bit."

"Are you sure?" Iris looks doubtful. "It doesn't seem safe to leave you alone – it's getting really late."

"I'll be fine." Morgana gives Iris a tight smile. "Art and the others are here, aren't they? I'll leave with them."

"It *hurts*," groans Lettie. "It hurts *so* much."

Iris glances at her, clearly torn.

"I'll text you when I'm home, OK?" Morgana makes a shooing gesture with her hands. "Now take that girl home before she needs airlifting out of here."

With one last worried look, Iris turns and drags a clearly overdramatic Lettie across the sand in the direction of the sheep path. Morgana watches until she's sure that they've gone and then steps out of the light of the bonfire, finding the dark shadows of the cliffs more fitting for her mood. Iris was right. It isn't safe to leave Morgana alone – but it isn't Morgana who she should be worried about.

She needs to work out how to get revenge on Lance. She has power, she knows that, and there is no way that Lance should have been able to do that jump. It's almost as if something stronger was able to counteract her hex. The image of Lance standing on top of Excalibur flashes into her mind and she shivers.

Something?

Or someone?

What if Lance has his own power and is using it against her?

Moving along the cliff base, she wanders for a minute or so until she reaches a shallow opening. It's nothing like her sea cave but it offers some protection from the wind that has blown up out of nowhere. She can focus here.

She climbs up on to a rock and sits with her back pressed against the cliff, enjoying the sound of the waves crashing on to the sand and the taste of salt in the air. Her hex worked with Maz. And with Lettie. So how come Lance didn't succumb to her magick?

The answer comes to her on the night breeze. It is *someone*, but of course it isn't Lance. He doesn't have that kind of power over her. It's her. She is the problem. She lost focus and allowed doubt to creep in, which ruined the spell entirely. And that's on her.

It's properly dark now, the night falling fast like a thick blanket cloaking the earth. She can hear kids partying and see the light of the bonfire. Their fun sounds silly, pointless somehow. There are better things that she could be doing.

Like seeing Celeste. She wondered earlier about leaving her a note at the Witch Tree, inviting her to join them tonight but then decided against it. It didn't seem like a good idea. She is two people. This new Morgana, one made of air, who lies in the woods and hangs ribbons in trees and shares her breath with a girl who tastes of apples. And another who is made of fire, who plots and schemes and seeks revenge for misdoings.

She isn't interested in Avalon Academy's opinion about who she dates and she isn't overly keen for Celeste to see the other version of her. She isn't lying to anyone – she's simply choosing which parts of herself to reveal and which to keep hidden in the shadows.

And it would seem that she is not the only one. Footsteps approach, and she shrinks back against the rock as they stop by the entrance to the opening.

"You're so beautiful."

It's him. Lance.

Morgana holds her breath in the darkness.

"One teeny tiny kiss," he says. "That's all I'm asking for. A kiss for being so brave."

"Brave – or stupid?" The reply is soft and teasing and Morgana instantly recognizes the voice.

Ginny. Art's girlfriend.

Morgana blinks in disbelief. What is Ginny doing here with Lance? Did Lance lure her over here somehow? Corner her? Well, he's messed up this time. She can help Ginny. They can hit him where it really hurts.

"Oh, sweetheart, I think you know the answer." His voice holds a smirk that she's glad it's too dark for her to see. "I'm one hundred per cent brave – unlike your boyfriend who's just pure stupid. Now where's that kiss?"

"Lance!" Ginny starts giggling. "Stop it! Someone will hear us."

Morgana claps her hand over her mouth to stop herself from shouting out as the truth hits her. Ginny has come here willingly with this loser. She's cheating on Art, with his best friend.

This is a plot twist that Morgana was not expecting.

CHAPTER 22

An hour later, the bonfire is nearly out and everyone is packing up. Ginny is hanging off Art's arm, laughing loudly at whatever he says like he's the funniest boy in Avalon. Morgana tags on to the back of the group and slowly they all make their way along the sheep path and round the headland, where the not-so-bright lights of the town are waiting to welcome them home.

They all disperse once they reach the Shack. Lance and Ginny live in the opposite direction to Pendragon Hall and so it makes sense for them to stumble off into the night together. Morgana watches them go, seeing Lance's arm snake round Ginny's waist when he thinks they are out of sight, and then she runs to catch up with Art and Vivi.

"I thought you'd gone," Art says, looking down at her

in surprise. "Someone said that you left with Lettie and Iris earlier."

"They left," she tells him, falling into step beside them. "I stayed. And I saw something I think you'll want to hear about." She turns to Vivi. "Can you give us some privacy?"

"Er, no she can't," snaps Art before Vivi can reply. "Whatever drama it is that you've created this time, you can say it in front of her."

"It's not *my* drama." Morgana is stung. "And I'm telling you this to help you, actually."

"Right, because you're so selfless." He rolls his eyes. "Go ahead – tell me whatever is so important it can't wait until the morning."

"Ginny is cheating on you with Lance." The words are out before she can formulate a softer way of saying it.

Vivi gasps, but Art doesn't even falter.

"Very funny. Jeez, what have you got against Lance at the moment?"

"I'm not joking." She stares at him in astonishment. "Your girlfriend is hooking up with your best friend."

Vivi looks at her reproachfully. "Why would Ginny do that? Especially with Lance, of all people?"

Ugh, Vivi is so naïve it's ridiculous. She'd think the best of a serial killer if they told her they were innocent.

"Shut up, Vivi. You don't know anything about anything so keep out of it." She catches hold of her brother's arm. "Art, I'm not messing about. Ginny is making a fool of you."

"No." He slows slightly. "She isn't. And you need to stop."

"I'm deadly serious." Morgana dodges round a lamp post. "I saw them tonight at the beach. Lance was calling you a loser and then Ginny kissed him and—"

"I said, you need to *stop*!" He slams to a halt and wheels round to face her. "I'm tired and it's late and I haven't got the energy for your particular brand of chaos tonight, OK?"

Morgana's mouth drops open. "So you're fine with being cheated on, are you?"

Art's eyes flash and now she sees the fury she glimpsed earlier.

"I'm *not* fine with you trying to sabotage the only good thing in my life," he yells. "I'm not about to let you take yet another person away from me. Do you understand, Morgana?"

The words slice into her heart. They've never been best friends, her and Art, but over the last four years she'd thought they had developed a kind of understanding. Sure, they annoy each other on a constant basis, but it's always felt as if they can find their way back to a place where they have some common ground.

But now she knows the truth.

I'm not about to let you take yet another person away from me.

He thinks she took away his mother.

He thinks she's trying to ruin his life.

He's right about the first but he's wrong about the second. Morgana is not about to be accused of a crime that she did not commit, not when the rap sheet is so long already.

"It's your funeral," she tells him. "I couldn't care less how much of an idiot you make yourself look, but don't come crying to me when you realize that I'm telling the truth."

"You're allergic to the truth," he spits at her. "Even Dad knows that. All you do is spread lies and hate."

And then he's gone, into the night.

"I'll go after him," Vivi says, casting Morgana a sympathetic look. "It might be better for you to stay out of his way for a while."

She races off, leaving Morgana standing on the side of the road and feeling more alone than she has ever felt before.

More alone and much, much angrier.

By the time she reaches Pendragon Hall, the anger has focused itself into a clear aim. Pulling out her Book of Shadows, she adds another name to the list.

Ginny.

Then Morgana lies on her bed, fully clothed and the windows thrown open to the night, listening to the distant sound of the waves as she lets her energy circle, weaving a plan out of shadows and salt air and the deep heat of her fury.

Ginny should have been loyal.

Lance should have been a friend.

Art should have believed her.

Vivi should be less irritating.

Now they must all pay the price.

"Are you OK?" Celeste looks at Morgana across the clearing. "You seem a bit off this afternoon."

"I'm fine." Morgana smiles at her. "I'm just not feeling the forest, that's all."

It's partly true. There is a strange energy here today, and the air feels tense and heavy. Morgana isn't sure whether it's emanating from her or the trees but, either way, she can't seem to settle and her brain can't focus on anything other than the spell she has decided to cast. Plus, she can't shake the feeling that she's being watched. It's a sensation that's been growing for a while, as if there are unseen eyes observing her every move, but whenever she turns to look, there is nobody there.

"I love hanging out with you here but maybe we can do something different next time?" She glances shyly at Celeste. "Like, a proper date?"

"I'd like that." Celeste grins back at her. "But for today, I've got a spell for us to try." She reaches for her bag and pulls out some pens and colourful strips of paper. "It's a communication spell, to aid our connection and bond."

Morgana sits up straighter and focuses all her attention on the girl in front of her. She doesn't want to ruin this precious time with Celeste with her own worries. And she's learning from her too – she knows she is.

"Right, so first you have to write your name on here." Celeste hands her a pen. "I'm going to do the same with my name and we're using green ink to symbolize friendship and good fortune."

Morgana carefully writes her name, pleased that she knew enough to use a red pen for power and strength when she scrawled Lettie's name for her bad luck spell.

"What now?" she asks, once her name is printed on the paper. "How is this going to work? And is the magick fast? What does it do?"

"You're always asking me questions! Well, this spell is a way of sharing some of the things that matter to us. But it's not about speed." Celeste hands her some more pieces of paper and then writes something on another strip, placing it down between them so that Morgana can see. "True magick isn't clicking your fingers and making something happen. It's about sending your desires into the universe and redistributing karma. A real witch works with the energies that surround us and that can't be rushed."

Morgana wrinkles her nose. "Some spells must happen quickly."

Celeste shrugs. "Only if that's what the universe is ready for. And only if you're prepared to pay the price of the magick. Now you can write anything you like on the paper and sharing the words will bind us together."

Morgana looks at the word Celeste has written.
Secrets

"Is that it?" Morgana looks up at Celeste. "It's just

a word. How is that supposed to help me know more about you?"

Celeste shrugs. "I guess it's a word that is important to me. Everyone has secrets and they don't have to be good or bad – but if they exist then it's for a reason. I'll tell you one of mine if you like?"

"You don't have to," says Morgana, suddenly panicked at what Celeste might be about to say.

"I once vowed never to return to this forest." Celeste glances around at the trees and then back at Morgana. "When we lived here before, my life was miserable and I thought that nothing good could ever happen in Avalon." She pulls her long hair back into a scruffy ponytail.

"So why are you here now?"

Celeste smiles softly. "That's a different secret." She nods at the Witch Tree. "I'm glad that I came back, though."

"I'm glad that you did too."

"Now it's your turn to write a word."

Morgana pauses for a moment, her mind whirring with questions. Why didn't Celeste want to return and what made her come back? She could ask, but perhaps she doesn't need to know. Celeste is right – everyone has secrets.

She rests the paper on her knee and leans over to write her own word, before placing it next to Celeste's on the ground.

Belief

"If we're going to tell the truth to each other, then we need to know that it will be believed. I told some people recently that a bad thing happened to me and they thought that I was lying – and that was almost as bad as the bad thing." She glances up at the tree branches above her, able to hear the tinkling of a bell but still failing to see where it's coming from. When she looks back down, Celeste has added another two strips of paper to the pile.

Listen

Trust

Morgana nods, picking up a piece of yellow paper.

Touch

Celeste reads it, reaching out a hand to briefly rest against Morgana's leg. They continue to write until all the strips of paper have words on them – words of openness and honesty, words of connection and belonging. They don't bother to explain them; the words themselves are enough.

Then Celeste picks up one of the pieces of paper and licks the edge before twisting it up and securing it in a loop. She chooses a different colour and threads it through, repeating the action so that the two loops are linked together. Morgana laughs as she realizes what she's doing.

"You're making a paper chain! I haven't seen one of these since I was a little kid!"

Her mind flashes back to a child's party.

Balloons and gifts and a big cake with eight candles flickering in the centre. Banners hanging from above. Games of pass-the-parcel and musical statues. Laughing children, squealing with excitement as they played on the bouncy castle in the garden.

Her, caught stuffing sandwiches, sausage rolls and a five-pound note from inside one of the birthday cards into her pockets by the birthday girl, who instantly informed everyone else at the party that Morgana Merrick was a thief.

Her, cornered by the birthday girl's mother, asking worriedly if Morgana was hungry and if she had enough to eat at home.

Her, cornered later by her own mother, berating her for getting caught.

Even back then, she wasn't good enough.

"Morgana?" Celeste's voice pulls her back. "Are you all right?"

She starts to nod, and then stops. This spell is about connection. Perhaps she should give it a go.

"I never had one of these when I was a kid," she admits, licking a piece of paper and adding it the chain. "But I think I would have loved it. It seems a little sad — it's just some bits of paper; not exactly a lot of effort for someone to go to, you know? I guess nobody ever thought I was worth it."

Celeste doesn't say anything, but when Morgana risks peeking at her she is relieved to see that the emotion flashing in her eyes doesn't look anything remotely like sympathy. Instead, there's an energy flowing off her that feels distinctly familiar — like the heat that bubbles in the depths of Morgana's very soul.

They continue to link the strips of paper until there

are only two pieces left – the ones with their names written on them. Celeste picks up hers and loops it through the first part of the chain before picking up the link with Morgana's name.

"My name goes here," she says, "and yours goes at the other end, with nothing but truth between us. It starts with me and it ends with you." She stands. "I've brought string so that we can hang it up."

Morgana has to stretch up on her tiptoes to reach the lowest branch. Celeste secures the chain in place and then bends to pick up the rose quartz from the ground, clasping it in her hands as they step back to admire their handiwork. The paper circles move gently in the breeze, the sun casting shadows of the loops against the trunk of the tree as Celeste completes the spell.

"Element of air, these words we share,
Keep us true, in all that we say and do."

She holds the rose quartz crystal in the air, letting the sunlight glint off its surfaces and then hands it to Morgana.

"To remind you that no matter what, someone will always think that you are worth it. I'm here for *you*, Morgana. It all ends with you, just like the paper chain."

Morgana holds the crystal for a moment and then puts it into her pocket. She feels its warmth the entire walk home.

CHAPTER 23

"I'm having a party here tonight," Art tells her, striding into the kitchen. "Don't tell Dad."

He hasn't spoken to her since Monday and her unwelcome reveal about Ginny and Lance. It's now Friday. Gordon has left for a business trip that apparently involves a weekend playing golf and steaming it out in a posh hotel sauna – despite claims of sticking around for a few weeks – and her brother clearly has plans.

Morgana stops juicing an orange and turns to stare at him. "Who's coming?"

"Everyone." He pauses for a second, as if he's debating his next words. "You can invite your friends but they're not my responsibility, OK?"

The doorbell rings and he darts off into the hallway,

returning a minute later with two women who start putting boxes of food in the fridge and on the kitchen counters. Morgana recognizes them as the caterers who deal with Gordon's work functions. A man enters the room with a crate of beer and she raises an eyebrow at Art.

"What's the big occasion?" she asks, laughing as he manoeuvres her out of the room and into the back garden.

"Shut up!" he hisses, throwing himself down on the outdoor sofa. "They think they're here for Dad. That's how I managed to get them to bring all that booze."

"Right." She takes a slurp of her juice. "That makes sense. But it still doesn't answer my question. What's all this in aid of?"

"Can't a man hold a party for his nearest and dearest without having an ulterior motive?"

"Nope." Morgana drains her glass and then sits down opposite Art. "Spill. What's going on?"

"Nothing is going on." Art smirks at her. "Nothing you need to worry about, anyway."

"There you are!" Vivi comes round the side of the house with her usual perfect timing, putting a stop to any further conversation. She holds up a large bag. "I've got the punch bowl and the bottle— Oh! Hi, Morgana."

"Hi," mutters Morgana.

Maybe she needs to make another magick jar spell and bury it by the back door. The first one doesn't seem to be impeding Vivi's ability to be a constant pain in her backside.

"Thanks for coming to help," says Art. "Shall we go inside?"

Of course he's getting his dogsbody to do all the work. If Vivi had some self-respect, she'd dump the punch bowl on his head and leave.

Morgana sighs. She really doesn't want to spend the whole night with Art and his friends without some back up.

You can invite your friends. Morgana wrinkles her nose, considering her options. The obvious choice is the remaining Sisters, but there's someone else who she'd far rather hang out with tonight.

"Hey, do either of you know the new girl in my year at school?" The words are out before she can stop them. "Her name is Celeste. She's got red hair and green eyes."

"Nope." Art shakes his head. "Doesn't ring a bell."

"How about you?" Morgana looks at Vivi. "Have you ever seen her?"

"I'm not sure." Vivi blinks rapidly, looking confused and a bit worried, her regular response to being asked anything. "Maybe. I don't think so. Sorry, why are you asking?"

Morgana shrugs. "Just a question, jeez."

"Right, this party isn't going to organise itself." Art nudges Vivi with his elbow. "Time to get to work."

He and Vivi disappear through the back door, discussing whether they need to push some furniture out of the way to make a dance floor. And that's when Morgana realizes that this party offers a brilliant opportunity to enact her punishment on both Ginny and Lance. The hex is ready to go, just waiting for the perfect time, and her helpful brother has handed that to her on a silver plate.

Art's head pops back out. "A word of warning for later — don't drink the punch," he tells Morgana with a wink.

Up in the trees, a raven caws.

She usually prefers to prepare herself before casting a hex, but Morgana hasn't got enough time to worry about that right now. She and Celeste have their first proper date this afternoon — and, after enthusiastically assuring the other girl that she will arrange all the details, Morgana is freaking the hell out. She's already wasted the last hour and still has nothing good to show for it.

"Maybe we could go for a walk?" she mutters to herself, pacing her bedroom floor. "No, too boring. OK, how about the cinema? No, she'll hate being stuck indoors all afternoon. God, why is this so hard?"

"You talking to yourself in there?" Art leans on the door frame, regarding her with amusement.

She gives him the finger and he turns to go.

"Wait!" Desperate times and all that. "I need some advice."

He spins back to look at her, his eyebrows raised. "About what?"

Morgana offers up a silent prayer to the universe and throws herself on his mercy. "If you were going on a first date with someone, here in Avalon, where would you take them?"

"Got a hot date, have you? Anyone I know?"

"No," she snaps, already regretting asking him. "Forget I said anything."

"Oh, come on, don't be like that." He puts his hand out to stop her closing the door. "I'm known for my excellent date recommendations – I can give you a few ideas."

"Seriously?" Morgana eyes him suspiciously.

"Seriously." He nods, and there is no hint of mockery on his face. "We're mostly set up for tonight – Vivi's gone home. Get me an iced coffee and I'll share my years of wisdom with you. Do we have a deal?"

She grins. "We have a deal."

"I don't really *do* the sea, but this is perfect."

Celeste lies back on the blanket and gazes up at the sky. Morgana moves the picnic basket that Art dug out from the back of a cupboard and lies down next to her, propping herself up on her elbow so that she can look at Celeste's perfect, gorgeous face.

"Your freckles look like constellations," she tells her, leaning over so that she can trace her finger against Celeste's skin. "You've got Cassiopeia on your left cheek and Orion just above your nose."

"Orion the Hunter," says Celeste lazily, closing her eyes. "I like that."

It's quiet on this part of the beach, just like Morgana knew it would be. The sheep path isn't frequented by the kids from Avalon Academy unless they're attending an

Excalibur jump, and there is nobody around to disturb them. She has to hand it to Art – the location was an excellent suggestion, as was the idea of getting Mabel/Mavis to pack her a picnic. A few crumbs and some empty containers are all that is left of the housekeeper's delicious homemade sausage rolls, strawberries and luscious lemon cake. What her casseroles lack in taste, her baking more than makes up for.

"I asked my brother if he'd ever seen you around," says Morgana, sitting up and shifting so that she can gently lift Celeste's head on to her lap. "He hasn't, though."

"That doesn't surprise me." Celeste's eyes stay closed.

Morgana laughs, starting to separate Celeste's hair into three strands. "Are you a figment of my imagination?"

"People see what they want to see," says Celeste. "And, believe me, I'm not usually what they're looking for."

"Then people are exceedingly stupid." Morgana weaves one of the strands over another, the beginnings of an intricate plait. "I only want to see you."

Celeste's eyes open and she looks up at Morgana. "That's because you are different."

"Tell me that you'll never leave me." Her words surprise her. She's been left before but she's never once asked anyone to stay. Morgana's fingers keep working on the red hair, twisting the strands together. "Promise."

Celeste sits up, patting her head to feel the plaits. "I promise that I'll be here as long as you need me." She swivels her head to look at Morgana. "That's the best I can do."

"Fine." Morgana nods, satisfied. "Well, I hope you're ready for forever then." She leans forward and plants a gentle kiss on Celeste's forehead. "Because I will never not need you. Now, let's swim!"

Morgana jumps up and quickly removes her t-shirt and shorts, already dressed in her bikini. She looks down at Celeste, who is leaning back on her elbows, a smile playing at her corners of her mouth.

"Are you not coming?"

Celeste wrinkles her nose. "No. I'm happier on solid ground. I'll watch you."

Morgana pauses for a moment, not wanting to leave but feeling the pull of the tide. Celeste nods encouragingly and the sea wins.

The water is cold against Morgana's skin. She moves fast, wading through the shallows until she's waist deep. Then she launches herself forward, her arms and legs moving powerfully as she swims further out. Only when she knows that the seabed is deep beneath her feet does she stop, flipping on to her back and allowing her body to float in the salty brine. The clouds flit across the blue sky and she lets her lungs fill with oxygen before exhaling slowly and letting herself sink below the surface.

Her eyes close and her hair flows out around her face. Her arms and legs become weightless and her mind clears of all thoughts. She is here, right now, and that is all that matters.

This is where she feels most alive.

This is where the magick happens.

Later, she sits huddled next to Celeste, the picnic blanket wrapped around them as the waves pound against the sand. The sound fills their ears and their hearts, watching the sun start to sink lower and lower in the sky. Once the temperature drops enough to pull goosebumps out of their skin, Celeste stands up and holds out a hand to Morgana. "We should probably head back."

They gather up the blanket and basket and set off in the direction of the headland.

"Shall we get a drink?" suggest Celeste, as they scramble down off the sheep path and on to the main beach. "Maybe at the Surf Shack?"

"No." Morgana drops Celeste's hand. "I don't want to do that."

"OK." Celeste says nothing more but the quick glance that she shoots at Morgana is laden with unspoken questions that Morgana doesn't want to have to answer. It's not that she's embarrassed to be seen with Celeste. She's almost sure that it's not that.

"I've got somewhere to show you," she says, pointing across the sand towards the far end of the cove, "and it's better than the Shack."

It's intended as an offering, an appeasement to make up for, once again, managing to disappoint. But it's also more than that. As they get closer and closer to the sea cave, Morgana realizes how much she wants to do this, how much she wants to share the things that matter to her with Celeste.

"It's this way." She leads the way round the cliff base, dumping the picnic basket on a rock. "Nobody ever really comes here. There are loads of stories about it being cursed, and terrible things happening in the cave."

Above their heads, the birds whirl in the sky like shadows. Celeste looks up for a second, and then back at the entrance to the cave, and for a moment Morgana thinks that she has made a terrible mistake. She shouldn't have brought her here. This place isn't like the forest, with its sun-dappled clearing and gently whispering trees. Down in this part of the bay, the sea is fierce and unrelenting, smashing against the rocks until it destroys them, just like it does to everything it touches. And that doesn't work for everyone.

"Can I go inside?" Celeste's request is almost a whisper.

Morgana smiles with relief. "Yes. But we haven't got long because the tide is on the turn and once it reaches the mouth of the cave then the only way out is to swim."

"How do you know that the tide is turning?" Celeste stares at the sea.

Morgana shrugs. "I can hear it, I guess. The wind picks up with the incoming tide so maybe it's that. I just always know."

Celeste's eyes flicker, reflecting the sea and the sky. "Sea witch. Why is the cave cursed?"

"Some people think that it holds one of the hidden entrances to the Otherworld." Morgana gazes at the dark entrance. "Legend has it that on the darkest, stormiest of nights, a young woman named Sibilla has been seen in the cave, holding an apple in her hand. If she offers it to you, and you accept, then that's it – you're trapped for ever in the land of the dead. Her revenge for the witch trials that killed her."

"Have you ever seen her?"

"No."

It's the truth – at least she's almost sure it is. Whatever or whoever she saw in the cave, reaching towards Lance's shoulder that night, was almost certainly just a trick of the light.

But it's also why the locals don't want their kids playing on this part of the beach. It's not just the fact that Alice disappeared here. The fear of the sea witch who lurks in the cave is woven into the fabric of Avalon. Morgana sometimes wonders if Sibilla was the last thing that Alice saw. Whether perhaps Alice took the apple from Sibilla's outstretched hand.

Morgana reaches for Celeste and together they walk forward. And then Morgana stops.

She thinks of Alice alone on the path. Of Lance stepping out of the shadows.

"I'm sorry," she tells Celeste. "I thought I could do this but I can't."

"It's OK." Celeste's mouth says one thing but her eyes are telling a different story. "Let's just go." She turns to walk away but Morgana pulls her back.

"It's not you," she says. "Really. Something happened

to me here and I haven't been back since." She hesitates, unsure how much she should share. "I thought coming here with you would make it better but I think the cave is ruined for me now."

Celeste looks at her for a long moment.

"Then we won't go inside," she agrees. "But maybe we can do something to get rid of the negative energy around here."

Morgana sinks on to the sand at the cave entrance. "What did you have in mind?" she asks, but Celeste is already wandering around the various rocks and pools and ledges that line this part of the cliffs, searching for whatever it is that she needs. Morgana watches her, allowing the presence of the cave to warm her back. She might not be able to go in there now, with Celeste, but she already knows that she'll be back. Anyway, who are they to determine whether an energy is good or bad? Morgana is starting to think that energy just *is*.

Celeste eventually returns with handfuls of shells that she tips on to the sand at Morgana's feet. Then she sits opposite her, pulling a sharpie out of her rucksack and selecting one of the flatter shells.

"I'm making you your own sea runes," she explains, when she sees Morgana staring at her quizzically. "You can leave them in the cave and use them to bring you good fortune."

She continues to work in the growing dusk, choosing shells and deftly drawing symbols on to them until there are twenty-four shells on the sand between them. Celeste picks one up and hands it to Morgana.

"This is Laguz," she says. "It represents water and flow and a journey to the very depths of the soul. I'll write you a list of what they all mean and then you can use them to create patterns that will cleanse the air in the cave and bring harmony and connection between land and sea."

Morgana holds the rune in her hand. It looks like an arrow with one of the pointed lines removed, as if it's telling them that there still might be some surprises along the way.

"Thank you." She smiles at Celeste. "They're really pretty. I love them and I'm definitely going to use them to harness the energy in this place."

Whether that energy is positive or negative remains to be seen.

"Can I ask you a question?" Morgana puts the rune down carefully on the sand. "What is this?"

"It's a rune." Celeste looks at her, puzzled. "I just told you."

"No." Morgana shakes her head. "This." She gestures to the space between them. "Us. What we're doing."

"Oh." Celeste shuffles forward, until her nose is almost touching Morgana's. "Well, I told you that too. It's what you need."

Her lips taste of sea salt and pine trees.

CHAPTER 24

Art's party is in full swing by the time Lettie and Iris arrive.

"This is amazing!" yells Lettie, pushing her way between kids who are gathered in every part of the ground floor of Pendragon Hall and brandishing her cast in the air. "Coming through, people!"

"What's the special occasion?" asks Iris, as they follow Lettie towards the orangery.

Morgana shrugs. "Who knows?"

She suspects the evening *will* be rather special, though. She has made her own plans, after all.

"I'll get you some drinks," she tells the girls, once they've settled themselves on the loungers by the pool. There are already kids in the water and Morgana can see a couple of empty beer cans floating in the deep end.

Gordon would go medieval if he saw his beloved Italian tiled pool being treated with such disrespect. She pulls out her phone and snaps a few pictures – it always pays to have some blackmail material in reserve.

Wandering into the kitchen, she pours some Coke into two glasses and then takes them back to the orangery.

"There's food in the dining room," she tells them. "I'll be back in a bit, OK?"

Lettie is already giggling hysterically at the sight of one of the boys from their maths class stripping down to his boxer shorts. Her obsession with Art seems to have run its course.

Morgana slips upstairs and into her room. Everything she needs for her true-colours hex is ready – to take down both Ginny and Lance. Tonight, their real selves will be revealed. The string and the red rose were easy enough to procure, but she had to give a bit more thought to the personal items. She still had some of Lance's hair left. Ginny was a bit trickier. Luck was on her side, though; when Ginny was last over she took her earrings off before going for a swim and left them on the side. Somehow one went "missing".

Checking that the door is locked, Morgana stands in front of her shrine and takes a few grounding breaths, visualising a protective circle around her. She closes her eyes and turns to face north, exhaling and asking the element of air to give her speed. Then she faces east, thanking the earth for the strength it sends. Spinning to the south, she asks fire for the courage to blaze through what needs to be done, and the west, where she sends her gratitude to water and the power she feels from the sea.

Opening her eyes, Morgana lights the three candles on the shrine and then picks up the red rose and the hair. She uses the string to bind the hair to the stem of the rose, repeating the same action with Ginny's earring. And then it is time.

Holding the rose up high, so that the candlelight flickers behind it, she starts to pull the petals off one at a time, reciting the words of the spell with every petal that is plucked and thrown on to the shrine.

> *You are revealed.*
> *You cannot hide.*
> *Your mask has slipped.*
> *Show what's inside.*
> *Your true desires*
> *Will all shine through.*
> *As these petals fall,*
> *Then so shall you.*

The petals now cover the top of the shrine. Morgana pulls out the last few and then scoops them up into her hands, bringing them close to her nose so that she can inhale the deep rich smell. It reminds her of a sunny day from years ago, when her mother took her to a botanical garden for the afternoon – a rare trip out when the temperature was so hot that staying in their tiny flat was unthinkable. She'd wandered off and somehow lost her mum and suddenly she was all alone, with no people to be seen. But the flowers were everywhere, their heady scent filling the air and making Morgana feel like she was suffocating. When she finally found her mother, she was laughing and chatting to a man she'd apparently "just bumped into" and hadn't even noticed that her daughter was missing.

She's always hated roses. They remind her of fakery and pretension, which makes it the perfect flower for this hex, which is guaranteed to make Lance and Ginny reveal their true colours.

Once the discarded petals have been tipped into a small charm bag, Morgana heads over to her mirror and gives herself a long, appraising stare. To the outside observer she thinks that she probably looks the same.

Perfect hair.
Perfect face.
Perfect body.
Perfect life.
And right now she's ready to be a perfect witch.

Downstairs, the party is increasing in both volume and intensity. Morgana stalks through the ground floor, looking for her targets – and then they're right there ahead of her. Together, of course. Karma knows what it's doing.

"Can I get you guys a drink?" she asks, ever the courteous hostess.

Lance turns to leer at her. "I've already got one." He holds a plastic cup filled with the punch up in the air and then knocks it back in one.

"I'm going to get a Coke in a minute," Ginny tells her. "Thanks, though."

"You should try this punch!" Lance wraps his arm round Ginny and she flinches at his touch. "Come on! Live a little!"

"You know I don't drink," she says, her teeth slightly gritted as she pulls away from him. "The one time I tried anything I got really sick – it's some kind of adverse reaction thing. Anyway, one of us needs to keep a clear head."

"Party pooper," he sulks. "Well, I'm going to go and find my boy then. No doubt he'll be up for some fun." He winks at Morgana. "Unless *you* fancy hanging out with me?"

"I'd rather die," she says sweetly, and he laughs, as if she's just said something amusing.

"Sorry about him," says Ginny once he's staggered off. "He gets a bit leery when he's had a beer."

Morgana snorts. "In that case I can only assume that he drinks beer for breakfast because he's leery from dawn until dusk."

"Yeah." Ginny stares in the direction that Lance went. "I think you might be right. I've always thought that he was a decent guy, but I'm starting to think that I might not be a very good judge of character." She turns back to look at Morgana. "Do you ever wonder if the reason everything gets messed up is because of you?"

"Because of *me*?" Morgana blinks. "What do you mean?"

Ginny shakes her head, laughing quietly. "No, not you! *Me*. I feel like I'm destined to constantly spoil things for myself, you know?"

"No. I've never felt like that," lies Morgana. She isn't sure whether the true colours hex has started to work or not but a deep and meaningful conversation with Ginny is not exactly how she wanted to use this magick.

"Sorry." Ginny exhales loudly. "I don't know why I said that. Just ignore me. I'm going to get a Coke. It's been a weird night already and I get the feeling it's only going to get weirder. Thanks, though." She smiles and for a brief second Morgana feels a tiny tinge of guilt for setting the hex in motion. But then Art stumbles into the room, his arm thrown round Lance and any regret she might have felt is evaporated.

"This dude right here is the best friend a person could ever have!" Art yells, his words slurring slightly.

Vivi appears behind them, looking as out of place as usual.

"No way, man!" Lance raises his now full cup and points at Art. "*I* have the best friend ever!"

"Nope." Art shakes his head exaggeratedly. "I definitely win. You are, without a shadow of a doubt, the best dude here." He drags Lance across to where Morgana and Ginny are standing. "And you, my gorgeous girlfriend, are the most exquisite, beautiful, attractive girl in the universe."

Lance nods enthusiastically. "She really is."

Ginny flushes. "How are you both drunk already?"

Art laughs. "The real question is, how are you not?" He thrusts a cup towards her. "Try my world-famous punch."

Ginny glares at him and turns to put the glass on the sideboard behind her. "No thanks. I value keeping my stomach lining intact. As you very well know."

"Leave her alone." Morgana has had enough.

"Yeah, leave me alone," echoes Ginny.

"Oh no, Art!" Lance clasps his hand to his mouth as if in shock. "We're going to get sent to the naughty step if we're not careful."

But Art disentangles himself and steps forward, reaching his hand out to take hold of Ginny's.

"Sorry, babe," he tells her. "We were acting like jerks."

Ginny laughs tightly. "Yeah, you were." She glances at Vivi, who is scanning the crowd anxiously. "Are you OK? You look worried."

Vivi winces. "I just don't want this party to get out of hand. And I'm a bit stressed about what's going to happen if my dad realizes that his vodka bottle has gone missing."

"You put vodka in the punch?" Ginny shakes Art's hand off her arm. "Are you insane?"

"It's a party, baby!" crows Lance. "Have a drink – it even makes Vivi look attractive!"

Morgana scowls and beside her Ginny gasps.

"Pack it in, dude," mutters Art awkwardly. "You're not funny. I'm sorry, Vivi."

"It's fine," says Vivi quickly. "He doesn't mean it – it's just the punch kicking in, isn't it?"

"It was a horrible thing to say," says Ginny. "And spiking the punch is irresponsible and dangerous. I'm going to throw it out."

"Stop freaking out," Art tells her. "It's fine."

"Stop freaking out?" Ginny glares at him. "Vivi literally just said that she stole her dad's vodka. Which" – she narrows her eyes – "is very out of character for you, Vivi."

Art starts laughing. "Seriously, it's OK. Come into the kitchen and see."

Art, Ginny and Lance walk towards the kitchen. Vivi hesitates and then follows and Morgana tags along, keen to see what Art is up to.

The kitchen is packed with kids. In the middle of the room the marble island is laden with a variety of Coke, lemonade and beer cans and in the centre is a large ornate-looking punch bowl, the contents of which are a noxious green colour. Beside the bowl is an empty bottle of vodka and all around kids are knocking back plastic cups of punch and getting rowdier by the second.

"Great party, man!" calls one boy, saluting Art with his empty cup.

"Don't peak too soon!" Art shouts back, and the boy laughs, dipping his cup back into the bowl for a refill.

"Don't mind if I do." Lance grabs a cup and fills it before downing the contents in one gulp. "Whoa, this is definitely the good stuff!"

Morgana shudders as he misjudges the distance and plunges his hand into the punch. If she thought it looked unappealing before, it's distinctly worse now his sweaty paws have touched it. "And what we're drinking is the real deal, baby!"

"Except it isn't." The corners of Art's mouth turn up and Morgana realizes that he's stopped slurring his words.

"It isn't what?" Lance upends the contents of the cup into his mouth.

"It isn't the real deal." Art is focused on Ginny now. "There isn't a drop of alcohol in that punch."

"What?" Ginny looks around the kitchen, at the kids dancing and shouting and stumbling around with huge grins plastered across their faces. "So all of this is—"

"Placebo effect," finishes Art. "They *think* that they're drinking vodka, which means they're acting drunk."

"But – but," Lance stutters. "What about the vodka bottle that Vivi stole from her dad?"

Vivi laughs quietly, clearly pleased in spite of herself. Morgana wonders just how long she's wanted to get one over on Lance. "You saw exactly that. A vodka bottle. It was empty when I took it – my dad keeps it for some weird sentimental reason, which is why I don't want him to notice that it's missing."

Lance stares at her.

Art pats him on the arm. "Sorry, dude. You believing that you're off your head is just the power of suggestion."

"Think about it," says Vivi, uncharacteristically brave. "Now you know the truth, do you still feel drunk?"

Lance scowls.

Morgana starts to laugh, and once she starts, she can't stop.

"So what *is* in the punch?" she asks through her splutters.

Art shrugs. "Orange juice, apple juice, grapefruit juice and some peppermint essence to give it a kick. Alongside a bottle of food colouring."

Morgana points at Lance, her hand shaking as her body rocks with laughter. "You got drunk on peppermint essence!" she crows, and beside her Vivi and Ginny start to giggle. "We've probably got some vanilla in the cupboard if you *really* want to get off your face."

"Shut the hell up," mutters Lance, an unsightly red flush creeping up his neck. He turns to Art. "Why would you trick me, man?"

"Don't take it personally, dude." Art claps Lance on the shoulder. "Just a bit of fun. Besides it was Vivi's idea."

They all turn to look at the girl standing next to him.

"It's for my A level psychology project," she says meekly. "It's an experiment to see how suggestible people can be."

"I'm not sure you can use it," Ginny tells her. "You have to ask permission from any test subjects before experimenting on them. We had that whole lesson on the policy of informed consent, don't you remember?"

Vivi's face falls. "So I can't even use this as data?"

Ginny shakes her head. "I don't think so." She smiles at Vivi. "It was a good idea, though."

"It was a *stupid* idea," growls Lance, who now seems remarkably sober. "And you totally should have got 'informed consent', whatever that is."

Vivi's lips quiver and Morgana rolls her eyes.

"Consent *is* important, Lance," she says coldly. "As you should know."

There's an uncomfortable silence and then Lance glares at Morgana.

"I don't know what you're going on about," he snaps. "But this party is crap. I'm going to get a beer and find some people who know how to have a good time, unlike you losers."

"Don't be like that," Art says, but Morgana can hear the lack of concern in his voice. "Look, let's all go for a swim to cool off."

"Fine," Lance says, sounding sulky. "But I'm not happy about being made to look a fool."

"Nobody made you look a fool," Art tells him.

"No, you did that all by yourself," adds Ginny, and Vivi snorts before trying to turn it into a cough.

Lance glares at them both and then stomps off after Art. Ginny throws a grin at the two other girls, and then the three of them follow the boys to the orangery where Lettie and Iris are now sitting with their feet dangling into the swimming pool.

"Where have you been?" Lettie asks, as she sits down next to them. "You've been gone for ages."

"Vivi!" Lance's voice bounces off the glass walls. "Come and take a photo of us diving in. You might as well make yourself useful."

"You don't have to do what he says, you know," mutters Morgana as Vivi raises her hand in acknowledgement of Lance's command. The two boys have already shrugged off their clothes. Ginny joins them in a bikini and all three now stand, ready to make their grand entrance into the pool.

"I know." Vivi gives Morgana a rueful smile. "But I don't mind. They're my friends, aren't they? Besides, I feel a bit bad about tricking Lance with the punch. He seemed really hurt and that wasn't my intention."

Morgana watches as Vivi walks round the pool. It's hot in the orangery and Vivi pauses for a brief moment to take off her hoodie before pulling her phone out of her back pocket. Art, Ginny and Lance are poised on the edge of the pool, and as Vivi approaches them, Morgana sees Lance's eyes dart to the side as he steps back.

A tingle of electricity shoots down her spine and she knows, without a shadow of a doubt, that her witchy radar is telling her that something is about to happen, something bad. She opens her mouth, not sure what to say but then, before she can issue a warning, Lance's arm shoots out and swipes Vivi into the water in one swift, fluid movement.

There is a moment of shocked silence and then Vivi

emerges, her face panicked before it sinks below the surface once more.

"She can't swim!" yells Art, and he dives in, emerging with a spluttering, coughing Vivi in his arms. Ginny scurries round to the side and kneels down, helping Vivi to heave herself over the side and on to the safety of the tiles.

"What the hell were you thinking?" screeches Ginny, once she's sure that Vivi is OK.

"It was an accident!" Lance crouches down beside them, his face contorted into an expression of concern. "I didn't even see her."

Vivi sits up, water streaming down her face. It's impossible to tell what is pool water and what is tears. "You pushed me," she splutters. "I could have died."

"You literally walked right into me," he tells her. "But you're OK." He pauses, glancing down at her and giving an appreciative smirk. "You look all right to me at least."

Someone sniggers and then a couple of kids start up a game of volleyball and the tension is broken. Vivi stands up, arms crossed defensively across her body and the suddenly transparent white T-shirt.

"I'm going to go and get changed," she says, her voice quiet. She turns to look at Lance. "You owe me a new phone."

"Yeah, he does. He's good for it, aren't you, dude?" says Art.

Lance nods, his mouth still quivering with laughter. "Sure. I'll get it ordered tomorrow. No worries – not for someone as gorgeous as you, sweetheart."

Vivi is shaking, although whether it's due to cold, fear or fury, Morgana can't tell. "You should just be thankful that Geoffrey wasn't in my pocket."

"Nah, I'm pretty sure that mice can swim," says Lance. "It would have been fun to see, anyway."

"That was completely out of order," Ginny tells him.

This latest stunt is clearly too much, even for her.

"Yeah, it was. Come on, Vivi," says Art, putting his arm round her, escorting her out of the room along with Ginny.

Lance dives into the pool and starts doing lengths. Lettie is talking about her missed modelling gig and how her agent thinks she might be able to go into modelling footwear instead. Morgana tunes out, thinking about what just happened. About the hex she set.

It seems that Lance has already been punished by making a fool of himself over the punch. And she wonders if Ginny has been punished too – by realising that Lance is such a jerk. They've both certainly revealed their true colours.

Maybe tonight's magick is over, Morgana thinks.

Maybe.

After ten minutes, Art appears in the doorway.

"Come on, Lance, I've lit the firepit," he calls. "We can chill out."

Lance pulls himself effortlessly out of the pool, standing beside Morgana as he dries off his hair.

"Get lost," she mutters, as he drips all over her. "You disgust me."

"Disgust is a strong emotion," he says, throwing his wet towel on to her lap. "Hard to tell the difference between something like disgust and, I don't know, attraction."

"Nope, I'd say it's pretty clear what the difference is," she tells him loudly. "Stay away from me, Lance."

Morgana throws the towel back at him and Lance grins, before walking off as if he's on a catwalk.

"What *did* happen between you two?" asks Lettie, leaning forward. "You can tell us the truth, Morgana. We won't tell anyone else."

Morgana takes a deep breath and asks herself if pushing Lettie into the pool with a broken wrist would be completely unforgivable.

"Should we go and join them in the garden?" asks Iris, as three kids dive-bomb the pool. "It's getting a bit wild in here."

"You can go where you want," Morgana tells her. "But I'm not going anywhere near that Neanderthal. Nor am I having any conversation about him."

They stay sitting by the pool, Iris and Lettie chatting about the kids that are currently engaged in making themselves look ridiculous, while Morgana focuses her energy on the hex that she has cast, trying to work out if there is still more to come tonight.

When the shouting starts, she tells herself that she isn't surprised, but her heart pounds in her chest as she dashes out of the orangery to see what's going on.

"Someone needs to call an ambulance!"

"What's happened?" Morgana pushes her way through

the kitchen and out into the back garden, pulling her phone out of her pocket as she goes, only to find that once again, the battery has died. The firepit lights up the section of patio where a throng of kids are bending over something on the ground and as she approaches, she can see that it isn't a something.

It's a someone.

"It's Ginny," says Vivi, looking up at her from where she's crouching beside the other girl, her face pale and drawn. Art is on the other side, speaking on the phone. "She said she felt dizzy and then she passed out." She shakes her head worriedly. "She wasn't even drinking; she just had a couple of glasses of Coke."

That's true – Ginny told Morgana that herself. She shivers in the night air. *This is it*, she thinks. The curse. She did this. At the same time she can't quite believe it.

"The ambulance is nearly here," Art says, his voice oozing with fear.

Morgana stands and retreats slowly, reluctant to encroach on the scene that she has created. Then the night sky is lit up with blue flashing lights and the sound of a siren and two paramedics are striding through the back door and telling everyone to get out of the way.

"What was she drinking?" Morgana hears one of them ask. "We need to take her glass with us to the hospital."

"She doesn't drink alcohol," Art tells them, suddenly sounding like a little boy. "Honestly."

"Just give us her glass, son," says the other paramedic, holding his fingers to Ginny's wrist. "We're not here to get you into trouble, but we need you to help us get *her* out of trouble."

"Where's Ginny's glass?" Art shouts. "It was right here. Lance? Vivi? Can you see it?"

There's a pause while they all hunt on the ground in the area round the firepit. Morgana watches as Ginny is loaded on to a stretcher.

"We can't find it." Art sounds close to tears now. "It was right here but it's gone."

"OK." The paramedics lift the stretcher. "One of you needs to come in the ambulance with us and we're going to need the contact details for her next of kin."

"Her next of kin?" Lance steps forward and Morgana can see that his eyes are twice their usual size. "Oh god, is she going to die?"

"We're going to take good care of her." The paramedics push past him, and the remaining kids part to let them through. It reminds Morgana of a funeral procession and she shivers.

"I'll go in the ambulance," says Art, his eyes roaming the garden until they land on Morgana. The fear and panic in them is visible, even in the dark.

She swallows and nods at him.

"I'll come too." Lance starts to follow the paramedics and then stops abruptly when Art yanks him back.

"No, you won't," he hisses. "You've done enough already."

They stare at each other for a few endless seconds and

then Art is gone in a blur of lights and noise. Lance pauses and then sprints round the side of the house, disappearing into the night.

"I'll get rid of everyone," Vivi tells Morgana, who can only nod again.

She stands there in the dark garden, watching through the brightly lit windows as the last stragglers, who have clearly stayed to witness the drama, are ushered out of Pendragon Hall. Then Vivi finds a bin bag and starts the mammoth task of cleaning up. Only when the deep cold that has permeated her bones makes it impossible to remain still, does Morgana stir. And as she moves towards the house, the sound of broken glass crunches underneath her trainers, echoing like gunshots in the dark.

CHAPTER 25

Morgana is still awake when Art gets home. Of course she is — she isn't a monster.

"How is Ginny?" she whispers, creeping out of her bedroom as he comes up the stairs. His face is pale and she can see that he's been crying.

"She's going to be OK." He looks up at her, his hand clutching the smooth oak banister like it's the only thing keeping him upright. "She woke up in the ambulance and then her parents got there, so I waited with them until the doctor came to tell them what had happened. And then they told me that it was better if I left."

"What did the doctor say?" Her heart is thudding at double speed and she leans back against the nearest wall, holding her breath.

"They found alcohol in her system." Art climbs a few more steps and then sinks on to the floor, slumped against the wooden spindles that connect the banister to the stairs. "She had a reaction to it."

Morgana exhales softly, controlling the rush of air that is suddenly desperate to leave her lungs. She didn't need to worry. Even the best doctors can't trace hexes.

"Her parents are furious." Art groans. "They all but accused me of giving her the drink. They blame me for this."

Morgana shakes her head and joins him on the floor. "I'm sure they don't."

"They do." His eyes flick to hers and then back to the ground. "I could see it on their faces. Even the doctor. There's no way that Ginny would have drunk it deliberately so someone had to have put the drink in her hand."

"But that doesn't mean they think it was you!" She's surprised by how much she wants to reassure him. "There are other people who it could have been."

"Like who?" Art leans forward and rests his head on his knees. "Who the hell would want to hurt Ginny like that?"

Her. Only she can't say that, obviously.

"The main thing is that she's going to be OK," Morgana tells him. "You said it yourself."

Art groans. "What a bloody mess. This wasn't supposed to be what happened tonight. I just wanted to—"

"You just wanted to what?" Morgana leans forward, sensing a plot. "What *was* supposed to happen tonight, Art?"

He lifts his head and stares at her with bleary red-rimmed eyes.

"I wanted to show Ginny that Lance can be a bit of a knob. That's all. I still don't believe that she'd cheat on me but I'm not stupid, Morgana – I know that he's constantly sniffing around her. Vivi was talking about some psychology experiment that she wanted to do and it gave me the idea for tonight. I knew he'd be the first person to fake being drunk. I thought it was going to be funny."

"Yeah, well, Lance wasn't laughing." Morgana looks back at him, her head racing with the opportunities that are throwing themselves into her lap. Karma clearly works in mysterious ways – Ginny has had her payback. Morgana didn't intend it to go so far, but perhaps there was a reason this happened tonight. Perhaps Lance's punishment is going to weave itself out of the ensuing aftermath and blame. At this rate she's not even going to have to say the words herself – Art is going to get there all by himself.

"No." Art frowns. "He wasn't."

Morgana inspects her fingernails, noticing with irritation that her right index finger has a chip in the gel. "Who got Ginny her drink?" she asks.

Art sits up a bit straighter and gazes over her shoulder, trying to recall the events of the evening. "I'm not sure. It could have been anyone."

"But it wasn't just *anyone* who gave her alcohol her, was it? Who do we know who might do something like this?"

She's taking a risk now, but she can see that she's hit a nerve.

Art pushes himself off the floor and starts to pace the hallway. "What are you suggesting?"

She shrugs. "Lance is your best friend, but he's also a nasty piece of work. He followed me to the cave that night at the beach and kissed me without my consent. This is exactly the sort of thing he might do."

Art spins round and stares at her, horror written across his face. "Are you serious?" he growls. "I heard rumours but … why didn't you tell me?"

Morgana's eyes widen, the tears prickling at their edges not entirely pretend. "Why do you think? You'd heard rumours, like you said, but you were only too quick to think the worst of me. You referred to it as *this story* that I was telling about Lance, so I wasn't exactly confident that you'd listen to me. And the people who knew about it, including your girlfriend, by the way, assumed that I was either lying or asking for it."

It's a master performance and it's not even that fake.

"I'm sorry." Art starts pacing again. "I'm going to make him pay. I swear it."

Morgana looks down at the floor, hiding her tiny smile.

The wheels are in motion. And Lance deserves everything that's coming to him.

The feather is on the front step when she opens the door late on Sunday morning. Just lying there, the blue black shimmering in the sunlight. Morgana glances around but there is nobody in sight other than the raven that seems to have taken up an almost constant residence at Pendragon Hall.

Once she's put the feather safely in her room, she heads out, knowing that last night's party is going to be all that anyone is talking about. Art left the house early with no indication of where he was going, but when she reaches the beach, Morgana isn't surprised to see Iggy parked up on the side of the road. The sea is where he always goes when he's feeling upset – it's one of the few things that they have in common.

The Shack is already busy. Vivi, Iris and Lettie wave her across to their table on the decking and Morgana slips on to a chair, braced for whatever conversation is about to erupt.

"Did you hear?" Vivi starts talking the second that she sits down. Out of all of them, she looks genuinely upset. "Apparently Ginny's drink had alcohol in it. Everyone knows that she's not allowed to drink! I've been texting and texting her, but I haven't heard anything back yet. It's all just so awful."

"It seems that Lance did it!" breathes Lettie in delighted horror.

Morgana raises her sunglasses and looks towards the sea. She can see Art out there, paddling furiously on his surfboard, but there is no sign of Lance.

"We don't *know* that yet…" says Iris slowly.

"Well, who else could it have been?" Vivi asks, sniffing loudly. "Especially after what happened to poor Morgana."

They all turn to look at her, and she lowers her glasses. "What makes you think Lance did it?" she asks. "Did Art tell you?"

Vivi looks awkward. "He didn't really tell us—"

"More like yelled it in Lance's face, before punching him," finishes Lettie gleefully. "Everyone heard. It's all anyone can talk about."

Morgana swallows back a smile and picks up the laminated menu, noticing the same sigil shape that she saw on the Tor, scratched into the surface of the table. Drawn by a chaos witch, Celeste had told her. They obviously aren't having much luck with their manifesting if they have to duplicate it in different places.

"I think I'm going to get brunch," she says. "Is anyone else getting anything?"

She doesn't want to be here. She wants to be lying in a forest clearing with the girl who makes it impossible to focus on anything else.

Iris frowns. "It doesn't seem quite right, does it? Us all sitting here in the sunshine while Ginny is lying in hospital."

Vivi's phone beeps and she grabs it, letting out a sigh of relief when she reads the text. "It's Ginny. She's home, but she won't be coming out for a few days. Her parents have grounded her."

"Well, there you go then." Morgana stands up. "She's fine and we can eat. It's what she'd want, you know?"

Lettie pushes back her chair. "Morgana's right. And I'm ordering smashed avocado on sourdough in memory of Ginny and her favourite food."

"She's not dead," mutters Iris.

"Thank god," says Vivi, putting her phone down. "If only everyone had listened to you, Morgana. About what Lance did to you. This could all have been avoided."

"I just think we should remember that people in this country are innocent until proven guilty." Iris looks up at the others. "We shouldn't go around spreading rumours when we don't actually know what happened—"

"I know what happened to me," Morgana reminds her coldly, moving towards the entrance to the Shack.

Together, the three of them stalk into the Shack, leaving Iris sitting alone at the table. Conversations hush as they walk past groups of kids, who look at them with a combination of curiosity, awe and a hint of fear. All Morgana's favourite things. They stand in the queue, all scrolling on their phones until it's their turn to order, enjoying the notoriety that last night's events has afforded them.

Iris is still at the table when they return. She looks up as they approach, her eyes wary. "I'm sorry, Morgana," she says quietly.

Morgana shrugs and considers Iris. She doesn't want anyone sticking up for Lance right now. In fact, quiet, gentle Iris has started to develop a way of stirring the pot in a manner she doesn't like. She can stop that, she thinks. If the last few days have taught her anything at all, it's that her power comes from deep within her. The crystals and the candles and the herbs are all useful tools, but what she possesses is more than that. She has manifested the downfall of Lance, and if Iris is going to get in her way, then that's nothing but a tiny hurdle to overcome.

"Two smashed avocado on sourdough and one French toast with fruit and crème fraîche." The waiter, a kid from Year Thirteen, places three plates down on the table. "I'll be back in a moment with your drinks."

"*Merci beaucoup.*" Lettie dips her head graciously at him. "*C'est très bon.*"

"You're not bloody French," hisses Morgana. "Just stop, OK?"

Lettie blinks but says nothing and they all sit in silence while the waiter heads back to the counter, returning with a tray of lattes.

"Did you want to order something?" he asks Iris, who shakes her head.

"I wonder whether the police will want to talk to Lance…" Vivi starts.

Iris joins in, offering a counterargument and Lettie talks over her, protesting. Nobody pays the slightest bit of attention to Morgana when she starts stirring her coffee.

Slowly.

Methodically.

Anti-clockwise to repel Iris's energy.

One, two, three times, stirring her intent into the drink. Focusing all her mind on making Iris stop talking and knowing, without a shadow of a doubt, that she will make it so.

CHAPTER 26

The history exam is easy. Morgana races through the paper, glad that her karmic debt for the hex on Iris, whatever it will be, isn't being paid in the form of a failed exam this time. She's keen to be done and back in the forest with Celeste.

Morgana hasn't told her what happened to Ginny at the weekend, although she's sure that the news has reached even the furthest corners of Avalon. It certainly made its way to the swanky hotel where Gordon was staying, thanks to the police contacting him about underage drinking at Pendragon Hall, which resulted in a heated conversation between him and Art when he stormed into the house early the next morning, shattering any hope that Art might have had about Gordon not noticing the catering bill. Morgana had stayed in her room. It wasn't her party, after all.

Once the exam is over, she makes her way out of the hall. Iris is ahead of her and she calls her name, only to see the other girl pick up speed and scurry between other kids towards the exit. Perhaps she didn't hear her? Or maybe the hex has kicked in and she's scuttling off back under the rock she climbed out from. Whatever the case, it is having the desired effect. If Iris isn't hanging around, then she can't be making stupid comments about Lance being innocent until proven guilty. Job done.

She pushes through the fire exit and heads round the side of the canteen, holding her breath as she walks past the bins. It's not the most aesthetic route to the block where her locker is situated but there's a shortcut behind the gym and she's unlikely to encounter anyone else out here, which is helpful. The last thing she wants to do is engage in any conversation about Ginny or the party. There are a few things that she needs to take care of before she meets up with Celeste, and the sooner she gets out, the better.

He's waiting for her. For a moment she hesitates and debates running back the way she came, but he's quicker than her and anyway she doesn't fear Lance. Not now she fully understands her power. Maybe she'll turn him into a toad if he annoys her too much.

The thought makes her smile, and she's still grinning as she comes alongside him.

"Hi," he says, sounding subdued. "Listen, can you to talk to Art for me?"

"Are you joking?" Morgana laughs. "As if."

Lance glares at her, taking a step forward. "I've managed to convince my parents and the head that what happened to Ginny had nothing to do with me, but Art won't listen. Which is unfair because it genuinely *wasn't* me that gave Ginny the drink."

Morgana screws up her face and holds out her hands, as if she's balancing the scales. "Should I help you? It's a real conundrum," she tells him. "I think … not. The thing is, Lance – you are a sad, pathetic loser who goes around behaving like he's God's gift to women when what you are is a lying, cheating, misogynistic bully who has betrayed his own best friend. And now everyone knows that."

His hand darts out and his fingers grip her arm. "Don't push me, M," he warns. "I didn't do this."

"Take your hand off me." Her voice is low as she tries to pull away, but his grip tightens. "You might not have done this, but that doesn't make you innocent."

"Just because I was flirting with Ginny doesn't mean that—"

"You've been hooking up with her." Morgana stares at him, her lips curled in disgust. "It's a bit more than flirting, Lance. And have you conveniently forgotten that you forced a kiss on me in the sea cave?"

"That's what this is about?" He looks at her in amazement, letting go of her arm. "One little kiss?"

And then he does something very, very foolish. So foolish that when Morgana replays the moment later in her head, she is surprised that she didn't strike him down on the spot.

He laughs. He laughs in her face.

She stands there, as still as a statue, watching him.

"You're tragic," he tells her once he's stopped laughing. "And I'll be friends with Art again, you'll see."

Then he's gone and Morgana walks quickly away on legs that feel suddenly wobbly, his finger marks red on her bare arm.

The corridor inside is empty, for which she is grateful. She's in no mood to explain her blotchy face and tear-streaked cheeks. She heads straight for her locker, unlocking the padlock with shaking hands and there it is. Another feather. Which means that the hex on Iris has worked. Morgana is still in control and it's all the sign that she needs.

It's time to end Lance.

And this time she's not going to take any chances.

CHAPTER 27

"What would you do?" Morgana asks Celeste. "What would you do if you wanted to stop a person from ever being able to hurt you again?"

Celeste rolls on to her side, bits of leaf caught in her hair.

"Who's hurt you?" she asks. "Tell me and I'll sort them out!"

Morgana sits up. This is what she was hoping to hear but she needs to do this right. It's unlikely that Celeste's definition of *sorting them out* is the same as hers. And she needs the other girl and her grounded forest magick. Dealing with Lance is clearly not a one-woman job if she wants the next hex to work. She's not had the best of luck cursing him so far.

"It's my brother's best friend," she tells Celeste. "Lance. You've probably seen him swaggering around the place, acting like he's a magnet for hot girls."

"Urgh." Celeste grimaces. "I think I know who you mean."

Morgana nods. "He's been causing me trouble and I need him to be dealt with."

"Was Lance the reason that you found it hard to go into the sea cave?" Celeste's voice is quiet.

"Yes."

Celeste pushes herself off the ground and walks over to the Witch Tree, putting her hand against the bark as if she's asking it a question.

Morgana waits.

And waits.

And waits, while the clouds scud across the sky and the leaves murmur secrets to one another.

The words, when they come, are sweeter than the sound of the hidden, tinkling bells.

"The Gretel sisters say that Lance needs to face the consequences of his negative actions.' Celeste turns to look at Morgana. "We must cast a bird's-nest spell, to return all his bad behaviour back to him."

"What does that entail? Will it be enough to get him out of my life?" asks Morgana, standing up.

Celeste nods. "How bad it is for Lance is entirely dependent on what he has done to others. The universe will mete out the appropriate justice."

Morgana smiles. "In that case it's going to be very bad for him indeed. What do we need? I'm assuming from the name that a bird's nest is somehow involved?"

Celeste grins at her. "It is, and luckily for you I know exactly where a disused nest is. Come on!"

Grabbing Morgana's hand, she pulls her out of the protective circle and together they walk through the woods, Celeste pointing out plants and gathering the items that she needs. Sometimes she seems to Morgana as if she is way older than sixteen. Sometimes it feels like Celeste has been walking these woods for centuries.

The bird's nest is the last thing that they collect; it's hidden deep inside the trunk of a gnarled oak tree in the depths of the forest.

"Why do we need this?" Morgana asks, as Celeste passes it to her. She holds the large, slightly scruffy nest gingerly in her hands, hoping that there aren't any insects hiding inside.

"Don't worry, it won't bite you," Celeste tells her. "And from the way it looks it hasn't been used as a nest for at least two years, so don't worry about that. We're not stealing anyone's home."

"What bird made this?" Morgana knows the answer even as she asks the question.

"It could be a raven." Celeste strides ahead, her hands filled with forest treasures. "Did you know that the collective noun is an *unkindness* of ravens? I think that's a bit mean – they get given a bad reputation when actually they're really smart creatures."

Celeste looks at the nest in her hands. Twigs and grasses and even a few bits of bone are weaved together to form a rough bowl, lined at the bottom with mud, sheep's wool and moss. Celeste is right – they are clever.

A noise attracts her attention and she glances up at the trees. "Could it not belong to her?" she asks, pointing to the raven that seems to be watching them.

"No." Celeste keeps walking. "This is definitely old."

"You didn't answer my question." Morgana hurries to catch up with the other girl as they re-enter the clearing. "What *is* a bird's-nest spell?"

Celeste steps into the circle and sinks on to the floor in front of the Witch Tree. Morgana joins her, putting the nest down carefully before them.

"There is an old English saying," Celeste says, putting the things she collected down on the ground. "*It's an ill bird that fouls its own nest.*"

"And what is that supposed to mean?" Morgana wrinkles her nose. "I want to put a stop to Lance, not faff about with sick birds."

"Firstly, *ill* means wrong, not sick." Celeste fixes her with a look, and then starts adding more moss to the base of the nest. "And secondly, what it means is that only a really evil person would hurt the people they spend most of their time with."

"Really?" Morgana pauses, her thoughts whirring. If that is the case, then almost everyone she knows is rotten to the core. Surely most people if they're going to be jerks, are jerks to the people that they're closest to?

"Listen" – Celeste's voice is serious – "everything we do comes with a cost. You know that, right? We can cast this spell on Lance, but we'll also have to pay the price. There are always repercussions, Morgana."

Morgana stares back at her. "I know."

God, how she knows.

"OK." Celeste nods. "We just need to line the sides with this blackthorn and then we can begin. Are you ready?" She places the dark twigs in the nest and then closes her eyes. Morgana copies her, listening as Celeste whispers under her breath.

"With this nest and these berries our intent is set.
Everything we give we get."

Something touches Morgana's hand and she opens her eyes to see that Celeste is handing her six dried juniper berries. She accepts them and watches as Celeste sprinkles her own berries into the nest.

"Juniper berries symbolize protection against evil," she tells Morgana. "I always use them in a spell like this, which is why I dry the berries when I harvest them every autumn. We want to make Lance experience his own bad behaviour and learn a lesson – but we don't want to curse him. Put your berries into the nest and then visualize Lance being made to feel the way that he has made others feel."

Morgana holds the berries for a moment and then tosses them into the nest.

"And now we just need to put it on Lance's doorstep."

Morgana blinks at Celeste.

"O-K?"

Celeste stands and pulls Morgana up. "That's the whole point of the spell. To show him that he shouldn't foul the place where he lives."

Morgana grins. "I'm down with that. I just wish I could be there to see his face when he discovers it, that's all!"

It's overcast as they leave the forest and head back down the track. When they reach the bottom, Celeste pulls Morgana to a halt.

"I think you should tell someone about what Lance did to you," she says. "Like your father or someone."

Morgana laughs. "There's no need, is there? We've cast the bird's-nest spell and he's going to get what's coming to him." She holds the nest aloft and makes her voice casual. "I'm going to drop this off. His house is just down here. Is it on your way home?"

She still doesn't know where Celeste lives, or who she lives with. Any attempt to question her ends up with Celeste making a joke, or pointing out a new and interesting plant, or, most effectively, distracting her with a kiss. Her newest tactic to find out more is to try to drop the topic casually into conversation.

"Everywhere is on my way home," Celeste tells her now. "But I have something that I need to do. Don't forget to leave your curtains open tonight and I'll see you tomorrow for our summer solstice celebration."

She gives Morgana a quick hug and then dashes off, leaving Morgana to walk down the High Street, pondering why Celeste is so reluctant to divulge any details about her life and why she's so fine with that. Whenever she thinks of her, which is a lot, it's always in the context of the forest or the Tor, not doing mundane things like homework or chores. That just feels too basic for someone who floats on the air the way Celeste does. And if Celeste's real life isn't something that she wants to share, then Morgana understands all about that.

The shops have closed and the High Street is empty, which is helpful. Not that the sight of a teenage girl carrying a bird's nest would raise as much as an eyebrow in Avalon, but still, she's keen to keep this aspect of herself hidden from public view. She walks to the end of the road and then, instead of turning towards Lance's house, she slips down the small side path that leads directly to the beach.

She didn't lie to Celeste. Not exactly. She *will* deposit the nest on his doorstep – but not before first adding an insurance policy of her own.

The sea cave looms before her, but she's been back since she tried to bring Celeste here and she is ready. Walking into the darkness, she grips the raven's nest in her hands, moving it so that the juniper berries roll around the base, faster and faster until she flicks her wrist and they all leap out of the nest, scattering on to the sandy floor of the cave. She has no intention of providing Lance with any protection against evil. Any protection from her.

The sea witch and the forest witch, that's what Celeste calls them and that's what gave her the idea.

Avalon is a place where all the elements converge.

Celeste is earth and air.

Morgana is fire and water.

She needs it all to stop Lance, and Celeste has just done her part. Now all that is needed is for Morgana to channel the energy of the sea. This, combined with Celeste's forest magick, will be more than even Lance can handle. She grins to herself in the gloom, already excited to see what the spell will deliver. What humiliation it will serve up to the boy who delivers it so freely to others. And this time she won't hold back.

The tiny rock pool is right at the back of the cave. It doesn't always have water in it – whether the cave floods or not is entirely dependent on the moon and the tide – but she has to believe that today it will be. As she approaches, the image of Lance lurching from the shadows flashes in front of her eyes, but she holds the nest and she holds her nerve and keeps on walking into the darkness. And then her eyes acclimatise and she can see that everything is just as she left it when she came down here earlier.

The seashell runes are laid out along the high ledge.

The rock pool is full of water.

The tiny glass bottle that she rescued from a junk shop is perched beside the runes.

Everything is perfect.

Moving quickly, aware that the tide is on the rise, she

fills the bottle. Then she sits down on the floor of the cave and listens. Really listens. She goes down below the roaring sound of the waves crashing on to the sand, down to where the sea tells its secrets to those who have the patience to listen. She's glad now that the hex didn't work when Lance jumped from *Excalibur*. The woods and their forest magick can have him.

She thinks of Lance appearing from the shadows of the cave and kissing her. Pushing Vivi into the water even though he knows that she can't swim. Kissing Ginny in the dark behind his best friend's back.

Let the Gretel sisters wreak their revenge on him and all like him, who judge and bully and condemn. Let him spend the rest of his pathetic life knowing exactly how it feels to hurt, to be afraid, to fear girls the way he has made them fear him.

Not that a little sea magick won't hurt, just to make sure that this time it really takes.

Holding the bottle in one hand and the nest in the other, she sprinkles sea water on to the twigs. Initially she'd thought that she would have to find some way to make him drink the water, and while there was a delicious irony to that, after everything that had happened with Ginny at the party, it also raised some logistical issues that she was struggling to get past. And then Celeste gave her the perfect receptacle. The bird's nest might not hold the water for long but she can see it seeping into the moss and sheep's wool that lines the base, and that's all that she needs.

It's getting dark by the time she stops outside his house. The lights are on inside and she can see his mother in the kitchen, stirring something on the stove. Lance walks into the room and she ducks behind a hedge, peeping through a gap in the leaves as he saunters up behind his mother and says something that makes her laugh.

She wouldn't laugh if she knew what her son was like. How he treated girls.

Crouching low, Morgana dashes up the path and places the nest right in the middle of the front doorstep. She can only hope that Lance is the first one out in the morning but it doesn't matter if he isn't. It's close enough to impact him regardless. Then, returning to safety behind the hedge, she keeps watching. She watches as Lance throws an arm round his mother and sticks his disgusting finger into the pot of sauce that she is making. She watches her bat him away with a tea towel, her face lit up by his presence. She smells the home-cooked food wafting out of the house and into the night and she hears the laughter, trickling through the letter box, as they prepare the table for their evening meal.

A perfect scene. A perfect family.

And she's about to expose him for the imperfect boy that he really is. The words of the hex, as she whispers them under her breath, will see to that.

In the darkness of the night
The raven is seen and the time is right.
This hex will shine a powerful light

On all the suffering and plight
That you have caused — now I bring the fight
To your front door, so that you might
Have your sins returned for my delight.
The moon bears witness as I cast this blight.
When a feather appears, the end is in sight.

CHAPTER 28

She wakes early, relishing the sight of the sun streaming through her window as she welcomes in the summer solstice and the day that stretches ahead of her. They have plans, her and Celeste. Swimming in the sea by the cave and then a picnic in the forest underneath the Witch Tree, followed by a solstice ritual that Celeste has promised is going to bring the sea and the forest together. Celeste is due to arrive for her first ever visit to Pendragon Hall in a couple of hours and it feels to Morgana like the longest day of the year is the perfect time to combine the two aspects of her life.

Morgana eases herself out of bed, going across the room to her walk-in wardrobe. The black feather tucked into the corner of her mirror makes her pause for a moment, her head whipping round to check that she's alone, but there's nobody else there. She glances into the glass and her reflection looks back at her, the Mallen streak seeming even whiter than normal against her black hair. Something big is coming – she can feel it in her bones, alongside a prickle of unease that she squashes back down.

The sense of uncertainty continues as she gets dressed and glides downstairs. She's not meeting Celeste for a few hours and has all the time in the world to enjoy preparing for their first solstice together. Perhaps once she knows what form Lance's karma has taken, she'll be able to relax and enjoy herself.

She sees Vivi standing in the back garden as soon as she enters the kitchen.

"Why is she just standing there?" Morgana mutters to herself, scowling at her through the window before opening the door and calling across the grass. "Did you want something?"

Vivi frowns, as if she's confused. She takes a step forward and then stops abruptly, before shaking her head and walking away. Morgana watches to make sure that she's really gone, noticing a flock of starlings flying in a V formation in the sky above Vivi's head.

She smiles. So that little hex she performed for Vivi has finally worked. She's never had a problem with crossing their threshold before. It's a timely reminder that her powers are growing, which bodes well for the bird's-nest spell that will pay Lance back for all the bad things that he has done.

Today really is going to be a turning point for them all and it's all down to her.

The first sign that anything is truly wrong comes from the sound of footsteps thundering down the stairs. Art bursts into the room, his phone in his hands and his face so drained of blood that he looks almost transparent.

"I–it's Ginny!" he stutters, brandishing the phone at Morgana. "Oh god, oh god, oh god."

"What's happened?" Morgana swallows her toast, struggling to move it past the lump in her throat that has suddenly appeared. *Ginny? She's done with targeting Ginny.* "Is she OK?"

Ginny has completely recovered. They all know that. She's not been allowed out of the house but she's been texting and posting on social media. The hex has been completed for her. She should be absolutely fine.

Art moves across to the sink and clutches the edge, as if he's about to throw-up.

"This isn't happening," he mumbles. "It's got to be a sick joke or something."

"Art!" Morgana resists the urge to shake him. "What's going on?"

Loud knocking interrupts her.

Art freezes as they hear Gordon striding out of his study and down the hallway, and then the sound of low voices at the front door float back to them.

"You need to tell me," Morgana whispers urgently, as multiple pairs of feet start heading towards the kitchen. "What's happened to Ginny?"

Art turns just as their father and two police officers

enter the kitchen. His eyes are wide and terrified and he's shaking his head as Gordon approaches him, a look on his face that Morgana has seen only once before. The night that Alice disappeared.

"Art," he starts, "I need to tell you something that's going to be really hard for you to hear—"

"I already know!" Art blurts, causing the eyebrow of one of the police officers to raise. "I got a text."

The second officer sighs and shakes her head. "We did request that nobody share the information. I'm going to ask that you refrain from posting online about this, while we're establishing the facts."

"These officers need to ask you a few questions," Gordon tells Art. "You're not in any trouble, son, and I'm going to be with you the whole time. They've already spoken with some of your friends. They're trying to piece together what happened."

"If we can go somewhere quiet?" The first officer glances at Morgana and then back at Gordon. "We can do this here or down at the station, whichever you'd prefer."

"Here is fine." Gordon puts his arm round Art's shoulder. "We can use my study."

"OK. Well, that works well for us," says the other officer, consulting her notebook. "We're going to visit your neighbour after this."

"Can I text Ginny back?" Art asks, his voice small. "Just to let her know that I saw her message?"

The officer nods. "Of course."

Gordon nods sadly. "The whole thing is utterly tragic, and for that poor girl to be the one who made the discovery? Well, it's truly awful." He releases Art and gestures towards the door. "My study is this way, officers."

The three of them walk out of the kitchen, followed by Art, his shoulders so slumped that he's almost doubled up on himself.

"What did she discover?" The words come out before she can stop them. "Art? What did Ginny discover?"

Art pauses, his back to her.

"Lance," he says. "She found Lance. In the forest, underneath a tree."

He turns slowly and Morgana can see that his eyes are glazed over, like he's trying not to look.

"He's dead, Morgana."

Gordon appears in the doorway. "Come on. The sooner you help the police with their enquiry, the sooner we can start figuring out how we can help that poor family."

He nods at Morgana and then they're gone and she is alone in the kitchen with legs that cannot support her weight and a head that feels as if it might explode.

Lance is dead.

Forget humiliation. Forget payback. She killed him. For real.

Morgana Merrick is a two-time killer, and she has never felt so terrified in her entire life.

CHAPTER 29

By the time the study door opens, Morgana has managed to pull herself off the kitchen floor and make it across to the table. She can hear the sound of the front door opening and then Art walks into the room, followed by Gordon, who heads across the kitchen.

"I think we all probably need a cup of tea after that," he says, filling the kettle with water.

Art slumps into a chair opposite Morgana. His face isn't pale now. It's flushed red, as if a bonfire has been lit inside him.

"What did the police say?" she asks quietly.

"They asked where I was last night," he tells her. "And they wanted to know about the fight I had with Lance at the beach the other day."

"I heard about that from the others." She gulps, feeling guilty. "Did you hurt him?"

"No!" Art shakes his head. "I was angry with him about what he did to you and what I thought he did to Ginny with the drink. I wish I'd left it now, but…"

"Do the police really think that you had something to do with this?" Morgana stares at him wildly. Framing her brother was not the plan.

But then manifesting murder had not been the plan — not really. Yes, she'd wanted Lance to pay, but not with his life.

"No, they do not." Gordon turns to face them. "Art has been completely truthful about the incident at the beach, but the facts speak for themselves. We have CCTV footage that shows nobody either entered or exited this house after ten o'clock last night and early forensics seem to indicate that Lance died sometime around two a.m. Whatever happened to that poor young man had nothing to do with anyone here."

The kettle starts to whistle and he turns back to take it off the stove.

Morgana looks at Art. He knows as well as she does that there are myriad ways to leave Pendragon Hall without being spotted on the security cameras. Gordon is wrong about that, just as he's wrong about this being unconnected to either of them.

"Drink this." Gordon puts two mugs of tea down on the table and then glances up at the clock on the wall.

"Damn. I'm supposed to be in a Zoom meeting with some investors." His eyes flit to Art. "Will you be OK if I'm in my study?"

Art nods. "I'm going to hang out here for a bit. I thought about going to see Ginny, but that feels a bit weird, you know?"

Gordon is already halfway across the room. "Great. Well, let me know if either of you need anything. Why don't you guys order some food in and try to relax? Credit card's in the drawer. Whatever you need, OK?"

Morgana stares after him. What are they supposed to do when what they need can't be bought?

"What happened?" she asks when he's safely gone. "Why was Lance in the forest?"

Art groans and puts down his mug, hands shaking. "Ginny phoned me this morning – she was basically hysterical so it was kind of hard to figure out what she was saying. Eventually I got the story out of her. When she woke up, she had three missed calls from Lance and a voice message asking where the hell she was. He said that he was waiting in the forest like she'd told him to. She tried to call him back but he didn't answer, so she snuck out to try to find him." He swallows. "I guess you were right about them seeing each other, after all. I can't believe I thought I loved her."

"Whereabouts was he? In the forest, I mean?" It feels wrong to ask but she has to know.

Art frowns at her. "I have no idea – the police didn't

say. Ginny was sobbing about a tree with weird stuff hanging off it, but I don't know what she meant."

The Witch Tree. Lance was found at the Witch Tree.

It shouldn't be a surprise but it is.

Art lowers his head on to his arms and Morgana can see his shoulders quivering. He mutters something into the table and she freezes, sure that she's misheard him.

"What did you say?" She leans closer. "Say that again."

"She said *there was blood everywhere*." A deep shuddering breath wracks his body. "She said that it looked like someone had bludgeoned him to death."

Bludgeoned. Just like the Gretel Sisters, all those years ago.

It was her who invoked the Gretel Sisters. It was her who put the raven feather in the tree and asked for their help. And now Lance has been killed in the exact same way that they died. Morgana's stomach churns and for a moment she sees black spots in front of her eyes.

There's a loud scraping noise as Art pushes back his chair and stands up. "I can't believe it." He gazes at Morgana and she can see the tears in his eyes. "He's dead. Lance is actually dead."

He shakes his head and walks slowly out of the room, as if it is taking all his energy just to remain upright. Morgana leans forward, resting her own head on the table. This is too much to handle on her own. She's done something horrific and she can't make it better no matter how hard she manifests.

Even she can't bring Lance back from the dead.

What she can do is try to mitigate any further damage.

She lifts her head and forces herself to stand. She wants to move quickly but her legs feel as if they are made of lead and it takes her for ever to climb the stairs and stumble to her bedroom. Her Book of Shadows is lying on top of the shrine and she picks it up, turning to the last page, the page with the list of names in purple ink. Ripping it out, she finds the box of matches before heading slowly into her bathroom, closing the door behind her to avoid setting off the smoke detector. And then everything speeds up with the strike of a match. It takes less than a breath to light the corner of the page and she holds it for a few seconds, the flame licking its way across the paper, eating the names until the heat reaches her hand and she drops the list into the sink, watching as the paper curls and turns yellow, then orange and then black, disintegrating into ashes.

If the list is gone, then maybe this will all stop.

When the doorbell rings an hour later, Morgana is lying on her bed. Slowly, feeling as if she's aged fifty years in the last few hours, she pulls herself up and plods down to the front door, holding it open to let her visitor walk through.

"Nice place." Celeste gazes around the hallway, taking in the antique furniture and huge chandelier that swings from the cathedral ceiling. "Hey, what's wrong?"

Morgana sinks on to the bottom stair and hugs her knees to her chest. "Everything," she mutters. "Me."

Celeste sits beside her and the cool touch of her skin against Morgana's arm feels simultaneously soothing and undeserving.

"What's going on? Talk to me, M."

"Hang on a minute," Morgana says, suddenly aware of Gordon and Art's presence in the house. She stands up and pulls Celeste back through the front door, walking across the lawn to the garden bench underneath the weeping willow.

And then Morgana tells Celeste everything she knows, starting with the arrival of the police that morning and ending with the discovery that Lance was found underneath the Witch Tree.

"It was me," she says, unable to look Celeste in the eye. "I wanted Lance to pay for the things he did and I went too far."

"What are you on about?" Celeste reaches out and puts her finger against Morgana's chin, gently turning her head so she can see her. "Do you mean the bird's-nest spell? Because there is no way that would cause a *death*. That's not how it works. It's awful about Lance, but this hasn't got anything to do with you, Morgana."

"No. You don't understand." Morgana pulls away. "I did this. I did all of this. I wasn't telling you the whole truth before. I created my own hexes and I've been getting more and more powerful but the results aren't always what I'm intending. I used a freezer spell to stop Maz talking about me, which worked just as I wanted, but the bad luck spell I put on Lettie made her break her wrist. I cast a true colours hex on Ginny and she ended up in hospital, which I never meant to happen. And now Lance has been found dead at the Witch Tree. All because of me." She pauses to take a breath. "You have to help me. Please. It was the combination of our magick that killed him and I need you to help me make this better."

Celeste stares at her for a long, silent moment that seems to Morgana to last for an eternity. The, slowly, quietly she starts to speak.

"Morgana, I need you to hear me. I don't know what kind of magick you've been doing, but I'm telling you right now you did not cause any of that stuff to happen."

Morgana stands up and starts to pace. "I thought you believed in the power of the universe. You told me that the Gretel sisters wanted to help. Was it all just a joke to you?"

"No." Celeste is quiet. "But I know that the sisters would never sanction killing, no matter what anyone had done. And I know that you don't have it in you to genuinely want to hurt others and that's where the true magick comes from."

Morgana snorts. "That's what you think. Close the gate on your way out if you're not going to help."

Celeste shakes her head. "I can help you, but not the way you're talking about. Is it just your group of friends who are getting hurt? If bad things are happening to kids in Avalon, then there's bound to be a genuine reason – and if it's magick then it isn't yours, I'm telling you that."

"There *is* a genuine reason!" Morgana howls in frustration, running her fingers through her hair. "It's because of me! I'm the one doing it. I had a list and almost everyone on it has been hurt."

"You're experiencing the negative energy you've put out there, returning to you three-fold," Celeste tells her. "But you didn't cause the bad things to happen, Morgana. That's not who you are."

"Art was on my list and he lost his mother, his best friend and his girlfriend – even if she isn't dead." She counts off her targets on her fingers. "Gordon lost his wife. Lettie broke her wrist and lost her modelling job. Ginny ended up in hospital and she and Art are probably over. Maz and Ro got publicly shamed and lost all their friends and now Lance is dead. The only person on my list who hasn't lost anything is my mother."

"She lost you," Celeste points out. "But that's on her. Just like all those other things are down to other people."

"I hexed Iris when she wouldn't stop going on about Lance being innocent." Morgana stops pacing and sits back down on the bench. "I manifested for her to stop talking and she's not been seen or heard from in days. Explain that."

Celeste shrugs. "I can't. But I can guarantee there *is* an explanation. Maybe if you speak to her, then she'll be able to tell you for herself." She stands up. "In fact, let's go and see her now. I can guarantee you that whatever the reason is, it won't be because of your hexing."

"Fine." Morgana grabs her phone. "But when it turns out that I'm right and that this is all down to me, will you help me then?"

Celeste nods. "I will always help you."

Morgana types out a quick text and watches as the three little dots flash on the screen, indicating that Iris is replying. Then she reaches her hand out towards Celeste.

"She's at the Shack," she tells her.

They walk down the drive, turning towards the town when the reach the gate, the raven eyeing them suspiciously from the stone pillar. They're silent as they head along the pavement and this time Morgana doesn't release Celeste's hand when they see other people approaching.

Instead, she clutches it tighter and tells herself that there is still a tiny sliver of hope.

CHAPTER 30

The Shack is as busy as usual for a Saturday morning, but the atmosphere is different. Bad news travels fast and as Morgana and Celeste push through the crowd they can hear snippets of conversation all bleeding into one another. Not that most people in Avalon have the faintest clue about how terrible this really is. They know Lance is dead and that the police are investigating but that's it.

For now.

"We're over here!" calls Lettie, half waving a hand in the air and beckoning them across to their usual table where she's sitting with Iris and Vivi. The corner table where, not so long ago there were nine of them gathered together. Now there are only four left and one of those four is looking like she would rather be anywhere else but here.

"This is Celeste." Morgana finally lets go of her hand. "She's with me."

Vivi nods nervously in acknowledgement and across the table. Iris looks down at her drink, seemingly unwilling to meet Morgana's eye. Lettie sniffs loudly, dabbing at her eyes with a hanky.

"How's Art?" Vivi asks once they're seated, her voice quiet. "I heard that the police went to see him this morning before they came to my house."

"He's not good." Morgana frowns.

"It's all just too awful." Iris's voice is hoarse, as if she's spent the morning crying. "I can't believe Lance is gone. I don't understand what happened. Could it have been some sort of accident?"

"That's what I've been wondering," says Lettie. "And why Lance was even in the forest in the first place?"

"The police told me that," says Vivi, leaning forward so that she can't be overheard. "Apparently he left a load of messages on Ginny's phone. He went there to meet her."

"Art said that too." It feels all kinds of wrong to be speculating on how Lance died when Morgana knows the real reason, but she can't afford to have the finger of suspicion being pointed at her. "They must have planned to meet up."

"That's the thing." Vivi lowers her voice even further. "I've been messaging Ginny and she says that she never arranged to meet up with Lance. Apparently she didn't even message him last night. But in one of the texts he said something about a note left in his letter box."

"So maybe they were going to meet up and then she changed her mind?" Celeste speaks up. She glances at Morgana. "Although that still doesn't explain what happened to Lance, does it?"

"Except that Ginny didn't leave a note for Lance." Vivi's hand flutters against her lips. "She says that she was at home. But *someone* obviously left it, right? Someone was at his house last night."

She's right about that, Morgana thinks. She had been there, watching Lance through the window. But she hadn't left any note.

"And there's something else that nobody knows." Vivi isn't finished. "What Ginny saw when she found him." She pauses and takes a deep breath. "Lance didn't just die, you guys. He had a massive blow to the head."

"Someone *killed* him?" Iris whispers, her hands starting to shake.

Morgana lowers her sunglasses. This isn't news to her or Celeste — but it's still painful to hear.

Vivi scrubs her eyes with the back of her hand and nods. "Yeah. Someone killed Lance and whoever did it is still out there." She stands abruptly. "Sorry, I need to go home."

The rest of them sit there as she pushes her way between the tables, shocked into silence by her revelation.

Minutes pass and then Celeste glances at Iris. "Morgana wanted to talk to you, Iris. She says that you've not been hanging out with them all for a few days. Can I ask why?"

"She knows exactly why." Iris doesn't seem scared now — she seems angry. "She's the one who put the photograph and note in my locker a few days ago."

"A note?" Celeste looks anxious and it could be Morgana's imagination but it feels like the other girl shifts slightly in her chair, putting some space between them. And Morgana knows why. Whoever killed Lance sent him a note too.

"What note?" Morgana snaps, her stomach starting to churn. "I didn't send you anything."

Iris puts her hand in her pocket and pulls out a photograph. "Yeah, right," she scoffs. "In fact, I was going to share this with everyone today. Show people what a bully you are." She slams the picture on to the table and they all stare at Morgana, who is blowing a kiss towards the camera. She's surrounded by them all — Maz, Lettie, Ro and Iris and it would be a cute scene — if their faces hadn't all been scratched out.

It is a horrifying image.

"But it just seems stupid now, after what's happened to Lance." Iris glowers at Morgana.

Celeste picks up the photograph and turns it over so that they can see the words written on the back.

Disagree with me again and I'll cut your tongue out of your mouth.

And under it a sigil. The mark of the chaos witch.

"That's horrible," breathes Lettie, narrowing her eyes. "Why would you send something like that to Iris?"

"I didn't write this." Morgana stares at the photo and the familiar sigil, and then across at Iris. "It's not even my handwriting."

"Whatever." Iris flicks her hand in the air. "So you got someone else to do your dirty work for you and then leave it in my locker. Same difference – the threat still came from you."

"No!" Morgana protests, her thoughts racing.

Could Celeste be right? Yes, Morgana had hexed Iris. But she hadn't written this. Nor had she sent a note to Lance telling him to go to the forest. Which means that somebody else had.

She stares again at the sigil. Whoever they are, they're using chaos magick to aid them.

"You can keep that." Iris nods at the photo and stands up abruptly. "And if you threaten me again, then I'm going to make sure that it's the last thing you do."

Morgana blinks, gazing at the girl who, until now, has only ever been meek and sugary-sweet.

"Right." Lettie joins her, a look of disgust on her face. "You've got a problem, Morgana. You're out of the Sisters for good and don't even think about trying to make it up with us."

Morgana studies the photograph, rereading the note as the two girls stalk away, arm in arm. There is something niggling at the edges of her mind but she can't place what it is or what it might mean.

"It wasn't me." Her brain is racing almost as fast as her

heart. All this time she's been so sure that her magick has been influencing the recent events in Avalon and she isn't quite sure what to think, now she knows that this isn't the truth.

She stares at Celeste. "I didn't do this."

Celeste reaches out and places her hand on top of Morgana's arm. "I know. That's what I've been trying to tell you. But, Morgana, that note is a real problem." She points at the sigil. "Whoever did these things, they aren't messing about. You need to stay out of this."

Morgana turns and looks across the sand, at the waves that crash against the beach, relentless and powerful.

It was never her. All along, someone else has been targeting the popular kids at Avalon Academy and unless she wants to be next, she needs to work out who it is.

CHAPTER 31

School is over. Exams are finished and Avalon Asks reveals that Morgana has been voted Most Popular Girl in Year Eleven. It's an accolade that until recently would have given her great satisfaction but that now seems petty and pointless. The summer lies ahead, endless, hot and dangerous. The forest is dead to them, along with the Witch Tree. The police investigation tape has been removed but Morgana has no desire to go up there. Not while there is a killer on the loose. She suspects that Celeste still spends her time amongst the trees, but that's her business.

The top of the Tor is busy today. Tourists flock in, unbothered by the death of a teenage boy in the nearby forest. There were a few days when it made the news, headlines screaming out LOCAL BOY BLUDGEONED TO DEATH and then a heatwave arrived and everyone's interest turned to possible hosepipe bans and fire risks.

Celeste and Morgana walk through the archway of the tower, stepping over the legs of families who are seeking shade beneath the old stone walls, and out to the other side, scrambling down the hill to the grassy ledge out of sight of the visitors. They don't speak. They know why they are here and there is no need for words.

Not yet.

Morgana begins. This is her spell. Celeste is here to add her power, but it's Morgana who must sort this out; she knows that. Closing her eyes, she takes a few deep breaths and visualizes a protective circle around them. Then she pulls a piece of string out of her pocket and starts to tie the first knot, adding a new knot for each line of the spell, reciting the words in her head where they are safe and private.

> One for the sun that shines a light.
> Two for the water that hears our plight.
> Three for the question in the air.
> Four for the truth that must be laid bare.
> Five for the flames that burn the liar.
> Six for the secrets in the fire.
> Seven for the blood, so thick and red.
> Reveal the person who wishes us dead.

When she's done, she wraps the string round her wrist and ties the ends together. A knot bracelet to symbolize the fact that she has carried out the knot spell.

Seven knots for strength and good fortune.

Seven knots to help her seek the answer to the question that nobody, not even the police, seems to be able to answer.

If Morgana's hexes aren't the reason for everything that has happened, then who or what is? And just how many of the accidents that have occurred in Avalon are they responsible for? Could whoever filmed Maz shoplifting the dress and put the video online have pushed Lettie down the stairs and given Ginny the wrong drink? Did they threaten Iris? And could they have sent the note that lured Lance to the Witch Tree before killing him?

Who is out to get them? And why are they targeting the exact same people that Morgana happens to have put a hex upon?

Could it really be coincidence? Or is it something even more sinister?

There are so many questions.

And now it's time to get some answers.

"You need to let it go now." Celeste's voice shakes Morgana out of her head. "You've put it out to the universe and there's nothing more you can do."

Morgana looks at her. "That's not what you said the other day. You told me that the only way I could make it better was to find the genuine reason for the attacks."

"You were distraught."

"A boy had just been killed."

"It's not a criticism." Celeste sighs. "I hated seeing you think that this was all down to you. But, Morgana, you saw the sigil on the back of the photo that was sent to Iris. A chaos witch can be dangerous. This is bigger than you. You have to leave this to the police."

"Right." Morgana stands up and brushes the grass off her skirt. "Because they're doing such a great job, yeah?"

"We don't know what they're doing." Celeste joins her and they start climbing back up the hill to the top of the Tor. "They could be close to finding the killer."

"They're not." Morgana doesn't bother explaining how she knows and Celeste doesn't ask. It's true, though. Gordon has friends in lots of different places and he receives daily updates on the investigation. To be fair, he's also done a lot to help Lance's family. He tried to get Morgana to visit with him when he took them a hamper of food, but she made an excuse about having a headache. The memory of Lance's mother, joking with him in their kitchen the evening before he died, is seared into her brain and she doesn't think she could bear to see the woman's eyes full of grief instead of laughter.

Celeste looks at her with concern. "Just promise me that you won't do anything stupid."

"Fine." She knows that crossing her fingers behind her back is childish but she doesn't care. It might not be her who has caused all of this but she's still involved somehow;

she can feel it. This chaos witch might be stronger than she is but Morgana still has power, even if it wasn't actually her magick that made all of the bad things happen. And she's going to use it find the killer.

She pushes the uneasy sensation that Celeste seems awfully keen to stop her investigating this to the back of her mind, along with the image of Celeste asking the Gretel sisters for advice on how to solve Morgana's problem. She can at least trust that Celeste isn't behind any of this. Can't she?

Back in her room, and alone, Morgana tips her seashell runes on to the bed. Celeste wrote her a brief list with their names and she found a more detailed guide in one of the many mystical bookshops on the High Street. She's been playing around with them more and more, asking questions and interpreting the answers and now, with her knot bracelet round her wrist, she's ready to focus her mind and start looking for clues.

She looks up at the ceiling and selects three runes at random, laying them in front of her and then looking down to see what has been chosen.

Thurisaz. Hagalaz. Algiz.
Boundaries. Disruption. Self-interest.

She repeats the words in her head, casting her mind over everything that has happened. There have been all kinds of rumours circulating about Lance's death, from misadventure to a terrible accident and a suggestion that he owed a debt to some out-of-towners. But Morgana doesn't believe any of that. What happened to Lance is part of the pattern of chaos amongst their group. Whoever killed Lance is the same person who has been targeting their group all along.

Boundaries. Disruption. Self-interest.

This wasn't done by a stranger. Whoever did this set out to hurt and humiliate their targets and it's someone who knows all the intricate details of their lives. Things that nobody else would ever know.

Someone who knew that Ginny and Lance were hooking up.

Someone who wanted Maz to pay for her crimes, Lettie to be punished for her disloyalty and Iris to be silenced.

And they're getting braver. What started with an online video has merged into physical harm, threats, making Ginny unwell — and now a dead boy.

And, however improbable it seems, this person knew about the hexes. Knew who was hurting or annoying Morgana. Knew exactly who was on her list and what she had planned for them.

This was done by someone who knows her.

What she can't work out is who. Or why.

CHAPTER 32

The thing about suspicion is that it moves silently. It oozes its way through the cracks in your defences and turns everything you see, hear or think into something dark and heavy, until you feel like you might drown under its weight.

Nobody is safe.

Morgana sits at her table at the Shack, hidden behind her sunglasses. And she listens. And she watches. And she waits. While all around her people discuss the end-of-year party and the new plan to turn it into a memorial for Lance.

The funeral happened yesterday. Morgana, dressed in black, stood beside Art and Gordon while the vicar banged on about what a "fine upstanding young man" Lance had been. She wondered if he had ever met Lance in real life, and then decided that it probably didn't matter. It's not as if he was going to stand up at his lectern and tell everyone that the kid was a knob.

The church was packed. Ginny was there, wearing sunglasses that hid most of her face, flanked on one side by Vivi and by Iris and Lettie on the other. The sight of Ro and Maz lurking at the back of the church, both dabbing at their dry eyes with a tissue, had caused Morgana to huff in exasperation, which she then had to speedily change into a cough when Gordon turned to frown at her. At one point, during the singing of "All Things Bright And Beautiful" (Lance's favourite hymn, according to the vicar) Morgana was sure that she saw a flash of red hair through one of the open doors. But when the funeral procession moved outside, the only thing to be seen was a raven perched on a tombstone beside a freshly dug grave.

The tears, when they trickled down her face, surprised her almost as much as the empty sensation she felt when the first spadefuls of soil were flung into the hole. Lance was a jerk and she had wished him to feel the hurt that he caused others, but there's a big difference between wanting and getting.

She knows that now.

The raven feather, waiting for her on her pillow when she got home from the cemetery, was a reminder that this is not over.

She looks around the Shack and considers the suspects. It could be Maz who is behind all this. She hated Morgana even before someone outed her crimes to the whole town and she was furious about being flung out of the group. And she and Ro have quite clearly teamed up – Morgana can see them now, inside the Shack, brave now that a bigger drama has freed them up to rejoin civilised society. Avalon Academy might be judgemental but even its students are prepared to admit that disloyal friends and petty shoplifting is not on the same scale as murder.

She sees Ginny huddled at a table with Vivi and a group of kids from Year Twelve. Both girls are getting a lot of attention right now, everyone keen to support them in their time of grief. Maybe it was Ginny who killed Lance. If she believed that he gave her the alcohol or was worried that he'd tell Art about their relationship, then she had motive. Or maybe Vivi was looking for revenge after he pushed her into the pool. Although that doesn't explain how either of them could mimic Morgana's hexes.

Perhaps thinking that this is all the work of one person is where Morgana's going wrong. Maybe it began with her telling everyone about Ro's betrayal and snowballed from there, like a sick game of dominoes. One wrong person wronging another and then another and another.

She shudders and sips her drink. It could be any of them.

Or, most terrifyingly of all, it isn't one of Morgana's enemies. It could be someone who knows her really well and believes that they are helping her. Removing her obstacles one at a time…

"Hey." A hand on her shoulder makes her jump. She really needs to calm down.

"Are you OK?" Celeste sits down opposite her. "How was the funeral yesterday? I missed you."

"It was awful." Morgana sighs. "I kept thinking that whoever killed Lance was probably there watching everyone mourn. That's what usually happens, isn't it? The murderer lurks somewhere to see the fruits of their labour."

Celeste frowns. "I'm sure that whoever did this is long gone."

"Are you?" Morgana removes her sunglasses and looks at Celeste properly this time. "What makes you say that?"

"I don't know." She shrugs and looks out at the sea, and Morgana follows her gaze. It's choppy out there today, the waves crashing on to the shore in quick succession like they've got something to prove. "Just a gut feeling, I guess."

"So you don't think it was someone right here in Avalon? Because I'm starting to think that this could be personal." She lets the words flow, making connections from all the mess. "I mean, whoever killed Lance could have easily had their own motive for sure. But what about everything else? The leaked video of Maz? Lettie's fall down the stairs? Ginny's drink? The threatening note? All these things happened to people who I had a problem with."

"What?" Celeste stares at her. "Are you still thinking that this is connected to you? Doesn't that seem a bit far-fetched?"

Morgana puts her elbows on the table and leans her chin on her fists. "Yes. It does. But that doesn't mean it isn't true. Put it this way – things have gone wrong for every single person who I put a hex on, which means one of two things. Either my magick caused this, which, as we've established, is unlikely. *Or* somebody is attacking every kid who I hang out with. But there are two people who haven't been targeted. Me." She pauses for a moment. "And you."

"That's true," says Celeste. "But I still don't think it means that these incidents are necessarily linked to you. And even if they are, then I really think you should leave it alone. For everyone's safety."

From anyone else's lips it would sound like a threat.

Morgana gazes at the girl whose fathomless eyes make her feel like she is lost at sea. Her theory is wild, but she knows that she's right. This is all linked to her; it has to be. The killer is clever and cunning and knows Morgana even better than she knows herself. Knows all her secrets and exactly how to play into her insecurities. And they're close. Really, really close. She can feel it.

Sitting up straight, she gulps in a lungful of air and breaks eye contact with Celeste.

"All I know is that I didn't film Maz shoplifting and I didn't push Lettie down the stairs. I didn't spike Ginny's drink, nor did I send Iris that photo and disgusting note, and I most definitely didn't bash Lance's brains out at the place we always hang out together." She takes a deep breath. "All of this began when you got here. And you told me yourself that you ask the Gretel sisters for advice."

Celeste's mouth drops open. "What are you saying?"

"I don't know," groans Morgana, already regretting her words.

Celeste stands up so fast that her chair tips over behind her. "Yeah, well, it sounds like you need some space to work things out. And I've had enough experience of being wrongly accused to last many lifetimes, so I'll get out of your way." Her face is completely blank, the way it was the first time Morgana encountered her at school, but her eyes are glimmering like a wave on the edge of breaking. "Have a nice life, Morgana. I hope you can take my advice and keep away from whatever chaos this is. May you get everything you wished for returned to you three-fold."

She storms off, and Morgana shivers despite the bright sunlight. She can hear the tide turning, bringing with it the promise of Celeste's parting words. She's either made the smartest move or the biggest mistake of her life.

And whatever happens next is not going to change the fact that she's just broken her own heart.

CHAPTER 33

"Have you got the fireworks?" Vivi is asking Art, as Morgana walks into the kitchen.

Morgana has to admit that Vivi has been a welcome presence over the last week. She's barely left Pendragon Hall and has been on hand with constant drinks and snacks, as well as staying up for hours every evening, listening to Art cry and rant and question again and again what could have happened to make everything go so wrong. Morgana has even felt grateful for her, which has been an unexpected emotion.

Not that she'd tell Vivi that.

They're throwing a memorial party for Lance tonight. The last few days have felt like being in limbo, hovering between the time before and the time after.

Art nods. "Yeah. They arrived this morning. I got Mabel to sign for the delivery – it's going to be perfect." He's put everything into this party to honour Lance. Morgana supposes it's hard to maintain a grudge against your cheating best friend when he's six feet under, or the girl who found him. He and Ginny have broken up, but they still text each other now and again, just to check in. Morgana imagines that the loss of Lance has given them a bond for life.

"I think Lance would have loved it," says Vivi, her eyes filling up with tears.

"He really would," agrees Lance. "You were right to suggest this, Vivi. It feels like the appropriate thing to do."

Morgana walks across to the fridge and opens the door, trying to choose between the bowl of freshly cut fruit or a pot of yoghurt. Then the distinct smell of sandalwood and vanilla wafts into her nostrils and she freezes.

"Can you grab me an apple juice?" Art calls. "And one for Vivi."

Slowly Morgana turns round but there's nobody there and the smell has faded. Appetite gone, she heads back to the table with the drinks and sits with the others. It's almost like old times, except for the fact that most of the chairs round the table are empty.

"Is everyone going to the party?" she asks, starting to peel an orange that she knows she won't be able to eat, but needing to have something to do with her hands.

"Everyone," affirms Lance. "It's all anyone is talking about."

"It's not going to like the usual end-of-year parties," Vivi tells Morgana, a warning in her voice. "So maybe remind your friends that they need to be respectful and not get too rowdy."

"Well, obviously." Morgana rolls her eyes. "It's a memorial party, not a prom."

"I just wanted you to know." Vivi looks at her thoughtfully. "I know you've been voted Most Popular Girl in Year Eleven and in usual circumstances tonight would celebrate that – even if most of the competition does seem to have been eliminated, one way or another."

"Whatever." Morgana pulls off a long strand of orange peel and throws it over her shoulder, idly wondering if it will reveal the initial of the killer. "I think I'll live."

"Unlike Lance," mutters Vivi.

"Vivi!" Morgana scrutinizes the peel, trying to work out if it's a random spiral or an actual letter. "I can't believe you said that!"

Vivi shrugs. "It's the truth, isn't it? He's dead and nobody knows why." She swallows. "Sorry, Art. I know today is supposed to be a celebration."

"It's OK," Art tells her. "We're all figuring out how to deal with this whole thing."

Morgana nods. "You're totally right. The killer is still out there. Any one of us could be next."

"Do you really think so?" Vivi's eyes widen. "God, I didn't even—"

"I'm going to get to the beach around eight o'clock,"

interrupts Art, shutting the topic down, and Vivi sinks back into her chair. "I want to make sure that everything is ready for when people start arriving." He looks at Morgana. "Do you want to come down early with me?"

They've been nicer to each other since the morning that Lance was discovered, almost as if they both know that there are few people they can trust right now.

Morgana shakes her head. "I've got some stuff to do. And to be honest I'm not even sure that I'm going to come. But thanks anyway."

Art nods and she's grateful that he doesn't challenge her. She's torn. One moment it seems unimaginable that she wouldn't attend the memorial party and in the next the idea of witnessing everyone mourning Lance makes her stomach churn. Especially when she hasn't ruled anyone out of the equation, and her feelings about Celeste are so confusing that she's given up trying to make sense of them altogether. But then perhaps a night like tonight, when the whole of Avalon will be at the beach, is the perfect opportunity to finally get some answers.

It seems wrong being up at the Witch Tree, especially without Celeste, but Morgana's feet have brought her here and she was almost powerless to stop them. She's not sure why the forest is calling her. When she left the kitchen, she'd looked at the knot bracelet on her wrist and had an overwhelming urge to come to the place where it had all started. And where it all ended. Now she's up here it seems like a stupid idea. She hated Lance, but, even so, being at the scene of his murder feels macabre. The police scoured the area before they reopened the clearing and she's not going to find any clues. And she already knows from her father that they've retrieved no evidence. But she wants answers and the Witch Tree feels like the place to get them.

She steps out into the clearing, feeling the familiar prickling sensation of being watched – but, as usual, there is nobody else to be seen. A flickering piece of police cordon tape, caught in a bramble, is the only evidence to suggest that anything sinister happened here. Although that's not entirely accurate. The large beech tree is evidence of an earlier brutality. Not that there would have been any investigation for the Gretel Sisters – not when it was the very people in authority who killed them.

Sitting down inside the protective circle, she pulls a small cloth bag and a book out of her rucksack. Then she tips the runes out on to the ground, closes her eyes and asks her question. "How do I end this?"

She circulates the runes with her right hand, moving them clockwise until she feels a particular urge to stop. She repeats this three times, selecting each rune and placing it in front of her before opening her eyes. Magick is her only hope now.

Eihwaz. Inguz. Nauthiz.

Morgana picks up the book and flicks to the relevant page for the explanation of the first rune, reading it aloud.

> If Eihwaz appears in a reading, be ready for a new situation to occur and for things to happen quickly. Eihwaz is the fire rune and the rune of progress, so do not be blind to opportunities that may present themselves. Have the courage of a hunter and stay calm – wait until your target is in your sights and then strike. Eihwaz may also represent a strong-willed woman and taking risks.

She pauses, listening to the wind rustling the leaves above her head and mulling over the words, before finding the description for the second rune.

> Inguz is the rune of potential. If you pull this rune, then it is a clear sign to not look back. The past is gone and it's what comes next that matters. You can live with regrets or you can look to the future, taking what you have learnt with you as you move forward. Inguz suggests that you have been struggling to solve a problem. Breathe and allow the bigger picture to form – when it does, the answer you have been looking for will be obvious.

Morgana laughs quietly. It's all very well for the runes to tell her to "breathe", but it isn't them that is dealing with an unknown killer who seems to have a hotline into her mind. She turns the page for the last rune, hoping that it will bring some clarity.

You are about to have a harsh dose of reality. Nauthiz, the rune of necessity, brings an unpleasant and possibly frightening revelation into your life. You need to remain strong and have trust. Someone close to you may not be who they claim to be, but friends and family will save you. Have strength. All bad things must end.

Morgana closes the book and picks up the three runes, holding them in her hands. The runes of progress, potential and necessity. The bringers of problems and solutions. She isn't sure what it all means, but one thing seems certain.

Something is about to happen.

And it's not going to be good.

Pushing herself off the forest floor, she starts to pace the circle, remembering what Celeste said to her on that first day. *It's not that it isn't safe for women and girls. It isn't safe because of the women and girls.* Maybe there's a clue in those words. Maybe someone should have told Lance that.

Not that he would have listened.

As she passes beneath the Witch Tree, Morgana tilts her head back and gazes up into the branches, staring at the familiar offerings hanging above her. The pentacle woven from twigs. The remains of their paper chain, partly disintegrated after the last rain shower, the words unreadable. The raven feather, still shimmering in the sunlight. And there, dangling beside the feather, a new talisman, glinting as it spins idly in the breeze, the now familiar sigil carved into the wood beside it.

Stretching on to her tiptoes, Morgana reaches up, her hands shaking as she struggles to grasp hold of the object. And she thinks that her heart might stop beating because this explains everything. She was wrong all along. Whoever murdered Lance hung this here and the police didn't even see it.

She was right about one thing, though. The killer has been in front of her this whole time. Like the runes said, *someone close to you may not be who they claim to be.*

There's rustling in the bushes at the edge of the clearing and then she hears the distinct sound of footsteps running away.

"I'm coming for you!" she calls, clutching the talisman in her hands, rage drowning out her terror. "I know who you are. And I'm going to make sure everyone else does too."

CHAPTER 34

The party is awful at the start, as Morgana knew it would be. Everywhere she looks, people are sobbing and wailing. One group is holding a vigil down at the water's edge, carrying candles and reminding each other of all the wild things that Lance ever did. The trauma and the drama have turned them all into actors, every single one of them trying their best to look suitably sad. They are genuinely upset; Morgana knows that. But she also knows that's not enough – they need to wear their grief like a cloak. Flamboyantly. Proudly. Loudly. Cameras on selfie mode as they snap pictures of their own tear-streaked faces.

Is it really grief if it isn't recorded on their profiles?

Things improve slightly once darkness falls. It's subtle at first, as if nobody wants to be seen having a good time.

And then Art lights the bonfire and the heat from the flames gives everyone permission to cast off their cloaks and reveal their true selves.

"To Lance!" Art hollers, pumping his fist in the air.

"To Lance!" the crowd shout back and then things start to hot up. The kid with his drum begins to beat a frantic rhythm and shoes are kicked off. Morgana sits in the sand, watching as they twist and turn, swinging each other one way and then the other, dancing their sadness out.

It feels like the night goes on for ever. Any other time she would have left, but the fireworks are planned for midnight and she has a plan of her own for after that, inspired by the rune reading and the discovery at the Witch Tree. But by eleven thirty, though, the thought of another thirty minutes in the presence of these people is enough to make her hot blood run very cold. There's only one person who she wants to see right now and she's not here.

But maybe she's on her way.

Maybe she read the note that Morgana left in the trunk of the Witch Tree.

She still doesn't know which way is up when it comes to Celeste, but she knows that she got it wrong. Celeste isn't a danger to anyone or anything, except Morgana's heart. Nobody notices as she slips away, up the beach towards the building that looms over the sand.

It's dark behind the Shack but Morgana can tell instantly that there is nobody else here. She moves forward slowly, seeing that the door to the small hut that stores the old surfboards is wide open. It's usually locked but the temperature has dropped and she wants somewhere quiet to wait until midnight. Glancing around, she creeps inside and settles herself down on the floor, her back resting against the wooden walls, the five short sentences that she wrote to Celeste repeating themselves in her head.

> I've figured out who killed Lance.
> I'm going to confront them tonight at the beach memorial.
> I know I'm sorry.
> I think I love you.
> I need you.

They were simple but honest; more honest than Morgana has ever been in her life and she's never written anything so terrifying. Taking a breath, she shifts into a more comfortable position and tries to settle her racing heart, letting her eyes focus on the faint light coming through the door from the full moon above. Whether she's more nervous about confronting the killer or confessing how she feels to Celeste, she isn't entirely sure. What she does know is that nothing will be the same after tonight.

And then there is a bang as the door crashes shut and darkness suddenly descends. Morgana hears first the sound of a bolt slamming home and then running feet.

"Hey!" she yells, rolling on to her hands and knees and crawling towards the door. "Let me out! I'm in here!"

The feet stop.

"Open up!" she orders. "I know who you are and we need to talk!"

There's a slight cough, and then the feet start moving again. Morgana freezes, the hair on her neck standing on end as she listens to the sound of someone prowling round the outside of the hut.

She stands very still, all her senses on overdrive. The footsteps stop and she waits, trying to decide whether they've gone or are lurking nearby. And then she cracks.

"Let me out!" Morgana pounds at the door. When it doesn't budge, she feels her away across to the opposite wall and picks up a surfboard, dragging it with her back to the door and slamming it as hard as she can against the wood. But the door refuses to move.

Then comes a series of loud bangs – the fireworks are starting. There is no point in shouting because the noise of the display is drowning out everything else. Morgana presses her face to a small hole in the door, watching. The explosions in the sky rival the explosions in her head as she tries to make sense of what the hell is going on. She can find just one explanation.

Someone saw her come in here and deliberately locked her in.

And the only person who has motive to do that is the very person she is tracking down.

The hunter has become the hunted.

CHAPTER 35

A firework whizzes overhead and Morgana flinches as it explodes nearby. She hammers again at the door and shouts until her voice is hoarse.

Another *bang*, this time much closer. And then she can smell smoke. Morgana yelps, spinning round to see smoke filtering through the celling slats in the far corner of the shed. Maybe the shed was hit by the errant firework.

Or maybe it wasn't an accident.

"No, no, no," she shouts, smacking her fists on the door and watching as flame starts to lick along the wall. She's going to die. She's going to burn to death like all the witches who came before her and nobody is going to know who she is. Nobody will plant a tree on top of her grave. People won't come from miles around to hang ribbons and bring offerings.

In death she's going to be the way she has been in life. Just not good enough.

Pulling her phone out, she holds it up in front of her and presses the side button. But nothing happens. Her phone is as dead as she is about to be. Of course it is. With a cry of fury she throws it on to the floor and then scrabbles in her pockets for something that might save her. But the only thing she finds is the talisman she plucked from the tree and the rose quartz that Celeste gifted to her that day in the woods. To remind her that there would always be someone who thought she was worth the effort.

Crouching down, her fingers sweep the floor, searching for anything that might help her as the fire takes hold. Smoke starts to trickle down like a waterfall and she clutches the quartz, her arm pressed against her mouth as it starts to fill the shed. She's dying and there is nothing that she can do about it. All the manifesting in the universe can't save her now.

Except this is not how it ends. It cannot possibly be how it ends. She is Morgana Merrick and she is everything.

Standing up, she puts her mouth to the small hole in the doorway and inhales the night air. The cold hits her lungs and kickstarts her mind and she suddenly knows what she has to do. Nobody is coming to rescue her but that is OK. She doesn't need anyone else. She just needs herself.

The rose quartz in her hand is jagged and hard. She grasps it tightly as she works it into the gap in the doorway. The hut is old and weather-beaten and no match for the sharp, durable crystal that represents healing and love and trust. The door starts to splinter as she grinds it away, the hole in front of her getting larger and larger until she can put her hand through and start to pull off pieces of wood, stretching her arm out as far as it will go, reaching for the metal bolt that is all that is standing between her and freedom.

And then her fingers touch metal and the door is released. Morgana falls out on to the sand, spluttering, choking, eyes streaming but very much alive, the precious rose quartz that saved her life still clutched in her fist. She rolls on to her back and stares at the fireworks that continue to light up the sky, trying to drag air into her burning lungs. She will never take another breath for granted, as long as she lives.

A figure looms above her, hooking hands under her arms and pulling her away from the shed, just as the roof collapses and the entire building bursts into flames.

"Get off me!" she screams, trying to scramble out of their reach.

"Morgana! It's me." Art. He's panting. He's clearly sprinted up the beach. "God, I saw the flames on the shed so I came down to see – but I had no idea anyone was in there. Are you OK?"

"What's going on?" Vivi races up to them. "I saw the flames and— Oh my god, Morgana, are you hurt?"

"We need to get her checked out." Art bends down, his face creased in worry, and Morgana recoils.

"Don't come any closer!" She scoots away from him, trying to put as much distance between them as possible. "I mean it, Art. I know what you've done and I'm going to tell everyone. It's over."

"What are you on about?" he asks, looking bewildered. Beside him, Vivi makes a strange strangled sound. In answer, Morgana delves in her pocket and then thrusts her hand forward, the wave pendant glinting in the flames, lying on her palm.

"I know it was you who locked me in the shed," she whispers, her eyes only on her brother. "I know it was you who lit the fire. And I know it was you who did all those other things too. I don't know why you wanted to hurt Maz and the rest of them, and I don't know how you could do what you did to Ginny and Lance, but it's over. I'm not going to let you hurt anyone else ever again."

Art rubs his hands across his face. He looks utterly confused, but that doesn't mean a thing. He's always been talented at playing the part of the good guy. "What are you talking about? I didn't hurt anyone and I sure as hell didn't lock you in the shed."

Morgana ignores him. Art has had everybody fooled, including her. Well, not any more.

"She's delirious," murmurs Vivi. "We should call an ambulance and make sure that she hasn't got smoke damage to her lungs or—"

"Back off, Vivi." Morgana glares at her, her words ice. "Even if he isn't prepared to admit to the other stuff, Art can't deny the evidence that he killed Lance. I found this at the place where he was killed. That's a fact."

"Morgana!" Art's voice is urgent and even though she doesn't want to look at his lying evil face, she can't stop her head from turning. Art tugs at the top of his T-shirt and pulls a necklace out from round his neck. "I'm wearing my necklace," he says quietly. "That isn't mine."

Legs shaking, she stands to join him. "But if it wasn't you, then it must have been—" She hesitates, and they both turn to look at Vivi, whose eyes widen in horror.

"Where's your necklace, Vivi?" Art asks her.

"I – I lost it." She stares at them.

"When?" Morgana fixes her with a hard look. "When did you lose it?"

"I don't know – a while ago." Vivi swallows loudly and looks at Art. "You can't seriously think that I had anything to do with Lance's death?"

"Of course not." His voice doesn't match his words and Vivi can hear it. "But we'd better tell the police that your necklace was at the crime scene. It could help with their investigation."

"R-right. Sure. That sounds like a ... like a good idea." Vivi steps backwards, keeping her eyes fixed on them. "We should call them once you've made sure that Morgana is OK. I'll wait over by the fire – it's so cold over here." She keeps walking backwards until she's far enough away to turn and run.

"It was her." Morgana takes a deep breath. "She did it."

"We can't know that." Art looks shell-shocked as they watch Vivi scurry across the beach, disappearing round a pile of rocks. "But all the same I'm calling Dad." He pulls out his phone. "He'll know what to do." His fingers hover over the screen and then he looks up, as if the magnitude of the whole thing is only now starting to dawn on him. "You could have died, Morgana."

Morgana pockets the necklace and then clenches her fist, the rose quartz still tucked inside the palm of her hand, stepping forward to test out the strength in her legs.

"Don't go anywhere," Art warns her, moving the phone away from his ear for a moment. "You need to get checked out to be sure you're— Hello? Dad? We need you at the beach. Like, right now."

He turns away as he talks and Morgana takes her chance. Her first few steps are wobbly, but then the adrenaline takes over and she's flying across the sand, so fast that her feet barely make contact with the ground below. Past the kids round the bonfire, where there is predictably no sign of Vivi, and then further into the shadows.

She knows exactly where Vivi has gone. She thought this would all end at the Witch Tree but she was wrong about that, along with everything else. Vivi has gone to the place where everything cursed goes. The place where this will finally be over.

The sea cave.

CHAPTER 36

The tide has turned. Morgana hears it before she sees it, slowly making its way up the sand. High on the cliffs above an unkindness of ravens swirl in the sky.

When a raven appears, the time is right.

"I know that you're in here." She swoops into the cave, any fear replaced with the fury that heats her soul. "And I'm not letting you leave until you tell me everything."

"You've got it all wrong." The voice is small and trembling and almost believable. Morgana walks forward until she's at the back of the cave, standing before the girl who is shivering and shaking on the rock in front of her. "I didn't mean to hurt anyone, least of all you."

"Liar." Morgana plants her feet into the sandy floor, ready to restrain her if necessary. "Try again."

Vivi gulps. "Can we go outside?" she begs. "I'd rather talk out there."

"No." Morgana scowls, pushing all thoughts of Lance and her similar plea to him out of her head. "We're staying in here until you tell me the truth."

"All – all right. But can we at least have some light? I know that you have a stash of candles and some matches."

Morgana is tempted to deny this request too, but she wants to see Vivi's face.

"Don't move," she instructs.

Quickly, with one eye on Vivi, she pushes the rose quartz back in her pocket and then retrieves the candles and matches from the tin she stores on a high cliff shelf, ramming them into the stone holes that act as candleholders. The cave is lit up with flickering flames and Morgana once again positions herself in front of Vivi, wincing at the sensation of heat that the candles produce, an unwelcome reminder of the burning shed.

"Right. Start at the beginning." She glares at Vivi. "I want to know everything."

"I don't know what it is that you think I've done." Vivi glances anxiously at the cave entrance, sweat plastering her strawberry-blonde hair to the side of her face. "I'm the victim here, not the villain."

Morgana snorts. "Yeah, right."

Vivi sighs quietly, as if she's weighing up her options. "Is there any chance that you might be interested in hearing about how none of this is my fault?"

"Er, no." Morgana takes a step forward. "Now how about you quit with the story time and start telling me the truth."

Vivi considers her, then nods, as if she's come to some kind of decision.

"Are you sure?" There is something that looks suspiciously like the beginnings of a smile at the corners of her mouth and her voice has changed from its usual quiet, meek tone to something more confident. Something harder. "You might not like what you hear."

"I don't like what I can see, let alone hear," snaps Morgana. "Now talk."

"Fine." Vivi rolls her neck around, easing the knots in her neck. "Where do you want me to start?"

"At the beginning." Morgana leans against the rock, rapidly losing patience.

Vivi smiles properly now. "OK, well, that's easy enough. This began with you, Morgana."

"With me?" Morgana stares, taken aback.

"Yes, you. I remember when you first came to Avalon. I saw the way you turned yourself from an unwanted, miserable, snotty kid into *this*." She waves her hand in Morgana's direction. "And I know it's all an act, but that's OK, because some of us were born for the stage. I watched you and I saw how you used your power to get what you wanted." Vivi laughs softly. "I'm a little embarrassed to admit that it had never dawned on me to improve my own lot in life until you showed me just what was possible. I really should thank you for showing a sister the way."

"I don't know what you're on about," mutters Morgana, feeling uncomfortable. "Tell me why you did it."

"Why I did what?" Vivi's hazel eyes glint in the candlelight. She's almost unrecognisable as the girl who has lived next door to them for all these years. "You're going to have to be a little more specific."

"Fine." Morgana shifts her weight to the other foot. "Why did you target my friends? What did anyone ever do to hurt you?"

"Are you serious?" Vivi stops smiling and sits up straight, seemingly growing in the candlelight. "Oh my god, you are!" She shakes her head in disbelief. "You've genuinely forgotten what it's like to be constantly at the mercy of a group of self-important, egotistical, privileged spoilt brats. Art was right – you're completely self-absorbed. You can't see anything beyond your own tiny sphere of existence." She laughs again, but this time there's no joy in the sound. "I knew it once I read your Book of Shadows, but it seems different somehow, hearing it coming out of your own mouth. It's not all about *you*, Morgana."

Morgana pushes herself off the wall and stares at Vivi, appalled. "You read my journal?"

"Well, duh?" Vivi snorts. "How else do you think everything that happened was so closely linked to your hexes? You gave me some good material. Damn, girl, you've got a sick mind!"

"What do you mean?" The balance between them has shifted and Morgana isn't sure how it happened. "This wasn't down to me. You did those things."

Vivi nods. "Of course I did. It was sweet, though, the way you thought you could control people with your little spells. But it was also helpful for me. You wanted Maz to shut up and she was an excellent starting point. I've known about her shoplifting for ages. It always pays to have some blackmail material up your sleeve – I believe *you* wrote that, didn't you, in your Book of Shadows? Anyway, it was fun punishing Maz. I realized that you were on to something with this hexing business – a way to mete out justice to those who hurt others."

Morgana frowns. "I was angry with Maz, but what possible reason did you have to ruin her? How did she hurt *you*?"

Vivi makes a huffing sound. "There she is again, Little Miss Self-Involved. If you ever paid any attention to anything that doesn't directly involve you, then you'd know that Maz took extreme joy in putting me down. Regularly. So I put her down. Plus, she was spreading rumours that you'd lied about what Lance did to you and that really got my blood boiling, you know?"

Morgana stares at her. "Why did you care what she said about me?"

"I didn't. Not really." Vivi pushes her hair off her face and adjusts herself on the rock, trying to get more comfortable. "But I wanted people to know the truth about Lance and what he's capable of."

"You mean that he—"

Vivi winces. "What do you think I mean? You're not that special, Morgana."

Morgana's stomach churns. "Why didn't you tell anyone?"

Vivi rolls her eyes. "Like you did, you mean? Yeah, well, I tried. But it turns out that not only did Ginny not believe me, but she also thought he was worth cheating on your brother for."

"Did Art know about Lance?" Morgana holds her breath, afraid of the answer.

"No." Vivi meets her eye. "Lance behaved marginally better when Art was around, which is why I tried to stay near him." She pauses. "Did *you* tell Art?"

"Not at the time." Morgana shakes her head and they both exhale simultaneously. There have been a lot of revelations tonight and Art is far from perfect, but the knowledge that he didn't know about Lance's behaviour lightens the atmosphere for a few seconds.

"But what about the others?" Morgana moves to the side, still keeping her distance from Vivi, who grins. She's underestimated the girl next door; Morgana knows that now.

"Well, you wanted Lettie to be dealt with next, which worked for me. She's always drawing attention to my *awful* taste in fashion and my *horrible baggy* clothing and, quite frankly, she's just mean." She holds up a hand to stop Morgana interrupting. "I enjoyed watching you believe that it was your magick that caused her to fall, when in reality it was just my foot. Plus, the sight of her sniffing around Art was starting to make me feel nauseous. She put her crush above her friends – very disloyal." Vivi looks at Morgana. "But you know that, right? Dragging you to the pool party, then ditching you with Lance. That's why you wanted her punished."

Morgana shudders. "I didn't say anything about pushing her down the stairs."

"No," agrees Vivi. "I came up with that all by myself. You're welcome."

"You're evil," Morgana mutters.

"Possibly." Vivi winks at her. "But it takes one to know one. What do they say? Birds of a feather flock together?"

"We are not the same," repeats Morgana. "And we are not flocking together."

"Whatever." Vivi is unbothered. "Oh, the ravens were a nice touch, though, yeah?"

"What?" Morgana feels like she's being bombarded with information and can't quite keep up. "The feathers were from you?"

"Of course they were!" Vivi makes a spluttering sound. "Oh my god, you really thought the birds were leaving you little signs of your almighty witch powers! That's too cute, it really is!" She cricks her neck again. "Nah, that was just me messing with you after I read that weird note you stuck in your book. *The ravens are all mine – they do what I want them to do.* I planted the feathers myself. It's a good job that you're a deep sleeper, that's all I can say."

"You came into my room at *night*?"

"At night. In the day." Vivi smirks. "I had to keep tabs on what you were writing in your Book of Shadows, didn't I? Do try to keep up."

"Did you read everything?"

Vivi's chuckle bounces off the cave walls. "Of course I did. I know all about your list of people who hurt you – and your fear that you were responsible for their downfall. I had rather hoped that you might be powerful enough to stir up some genuine trouble, especially when you joined forces with the forest witch." She wrinkles her nose. "You've got something, the two of you – but I guess that, even combined, neither of you have the energy that I can summon."

"*You* have powers?" Morgana whispers. "That can't be true."

Even as she says it, she knows that it is. The way that animals are drawn to Vivi. The way she sits on the outside of the group, always there but somehow invisible.

Watching. Waiting.

She stares at Vivi in horror. "What did you do?"

CHAPTER 37

"I didn't waste my precious magick on them," scoffs Vivi. "Anyway, I needed a quick fix and magick isn't good for that. When it became clear that you were useless, I took matters into my own hands. I handed Ginny the wrong drink to pay her back for cheating on Art, which I suspected but wouldn't have known about if you hadn't written it in your Book of Shadows, so thanks for that. And of course everyone suspected Lance."

"But you messed that up," says Morgana, fighting to regain some sense of control. "My hex was for Ginny to show her true colours, not end up in hospital."

Vivi makes a disappointed noise with her tongue. "I worked with what was available. Ginny was punished for being awful to Art, the one person who has ever treated me with any kindness or respect – there's no need to be so pedantic about it."

"I'm going to tell everyone what you've done," warns Morgana. "You're going to pay for this for the rest of your life."

Vivi smiles at Morgana. "Are you, though? You're my accomplice, Morgana. We did this together. You even broke the glass I gave Ginny – I saw you tread on it while I was clearing up, as usual. Destruction of evidence is a crime, you know? I couldn't have done it without you, babe."

Morgana's done listening to this. "You're not well," she tells Vivi, backing away. "Seriously. You need help."

"I had help," Vivi says, hugging her knees up to her chest. "I had you, Morgana. You were the inspiration for it all."

"Stop saying that!" Morgana shouts. "There's a massive difference between writing things in a book and actually going out and hurting people."

"Is there?" Vivi looks at her intently. "Even when you truly believe that the words you're writing have power?"

"It's not the same." Morgana shakes her head. "And what about me? You locked me in the shed and set fire to it. Why? What did I ever do to you?"

"You were going to ruin everything. I was there when you found the necklace." Vivi glares at her. "You shouldn't have pulled it down from the Witch Tree, Morgana. That was a gift for the Gretel Sisters, and it wasn't yours to take."

"You could have killed me!"

"I didn't, though, did I?" Vivi waves dismissively. "So stop your bleating. Anyway, I just wanted to stop you talking to Art before I could get the necklace back. I thought everyone would think that the fire was started by a firework, not this." She flicks her fingers and a flame pops out of a lighter that seems to have magically appeared in her hand.

"Oh my god," breathes Morgana. "You really tried to kill me – for *this*?"

She holds the chain out in front of her and Vivi visibly flinches.

"It's not about the necklace, though, is it? It's about what the necklace means."

"It means you killed Lance," says Morgana.

"I wanted your plan for Lance to be enough," she says, quieter now, and Morgana has to strain to hear her. "I wasn't planning on killing him. But I wanted him punished and I knew he wouldn't be. He always gets away with everything."

"The photograph of us all in Iris's locker." Morgana shivers. "I knew that I recognized it. *You* took that picture – last Christmas."

"I did." Vivi nods. "By that point I was honestly amazed that you hadn't worked out it was me. I was getting a bit bored of having to sneak into Pendragon Hall all the time." Her mouth turns up at the corners. "Good job we all know how to get in and out undetected, huh? Anyway,

I didn't want Iris sticking up for Lance. And then I had to end him."

"What did you do?" Morgana knows the answer. What she doesn't know is why she's asking the question when she should be getting away.

Vivi sighs. "I put the note through Lance's letter box," she says. "I had to wait, obviously, while you delivered the bird's-nest spell to his doorstep and muttered your ineffective incantation. Then I left the note – supposedly from Ginny – and went to the Witch Tree to wait." She shakes her head. "That spell was never going to work for you, by the way. The ravens are mine to command, not yours. You've got so much to learn, Morgana. Celeste tried to tell you; I heard her. You can use your magick for revenge, but it's subtle. It takes time. The magick is all about karmic redistribution – it's about give and take. It doesn't happen just because you want it to. There's a whole world of difference between *want* and *need*, you know. That's why I had to use real-world solutions. We both wanted fast action and I provided it."

"How did you know about the tree?"

"Come on." Vivi sighs. "I can't be expected to do all the legwork here, Morgana."

"You followed Celeste and me."

The feeling of being watched. The prickling sensation of eyes upon her.

Vivi flicks her hand in the air. "I've been visiting the Witch Tree for years. You and your girlfriend imposed on *my* space, not the other way round. Anyway, that's not important. I waited until Lance arrived. He was confused at first – he was expecting Ginny, after all – but then I confronted him about the way he was treating me and everyone else. I told him that I'd had enough." Her eyes glaze over, as if she's reliving the moment. "I said that I'd tell Art about what a jerk he is and about him cheating with Ginny, but he just laughed at me. He told me that that I'm a joke." She sniffs loudly. "He said that I should be grateful that any of you let me hang around and that you all laugh at me behind my back."

"That was a terrible thing to say," Morgana says carefully. "But it's not exactly a motive for murder, is it?"

"And then he said he'd do me a favour and kiss me, as I so clearly wanted his attention. I didn't mean to kill him." Vivi looks at her, suddenly sounding desperate and upset. "It's just that the awfulness of what he was saying took my breath away. So I took his breath away. Permanently."

CHAPTER 38

Morgana feels water against her feet and when she looks down, sees that the tide is sweeping into the cave, dark, cold and urgent.

They need to leave.

"We have to get out of here. Come on."

Vivi looks down, only now noticing that the cave floor is filling with rapidly rising water. "Morgana, you do know that I can't swim, don't you?" Her breathing speeds up and she looks pale in the flickering of the candlelight.

"Everyone knows that. I'll help you, but we have to go now."

"You'd really help me?" asks Vivi. "After everything I've just told you? Even though you know that I hate you all – that I've always hated you all." She laughs quietly, any vulnerability vanishing. "Wow. You really don't have any backbone, do you? No wonder everyone you care about always ends up leaving you."

The fear and rage sit like a lead block in the pit of Morgana's stomach, extinguishing any brief solidarity that she might have felt with the other girl. "You don't know anything about me," she snarls.

"Do you really believe that?" Vivi sounds genuinely intrigued. "Of course I know you. We're the same, Morgana."

"We are nothing like the same," roars Morgana, clenching her fists. "I haven't gone around hurting everyone, have I?"

"Haven't you?"

"Fine. One more word and I really will leave you here to drown." Morgana turns to look at the cave entrance. "In five minutes this cave is going to be six feet deep in water. It's your funeral, Vivi. Now let's go!"

"They used to drown witches, you know." Vivi leans forward, perched on her rock as the water starts to lap at the edges. "If they died, then they were innocent. Which means that I'm going to live."

"Stop this," shouts Morgana. "You genuinely think that you can sit here while the cave floods and then walk out afterwards?"

"Why not?" Vivi yells back, over the sound of rushing water. "They used to burn witches too, and you walked out of the burning shed just fine, didn't you?"

The water is almost at chest level and very soon it's going to be too deep to wade through. Morgana's a strong swimmer but she isn't strong enough for both of them. If she leaves Vivi here, then she's got a good chance of making it out alive. If she tries to save her, then the odds are not in their favour.

"Why do you think you have the right to judge me?" calls Vivi, panic in her voice now. "Which one of us has done the most damage really? You're as broken as I am, Morgana. We're driven by hate, not love – accept it."

Morgana hesitates. It's true that her power has been based on the cracks that she can feel deep within herself. But cracks can be fixed. Broken things can be healed – she has to believe that is true.

The water swells higher and she makes up her mind.

She reaches out her hand to Vivi.

"Come on!" she yells. "We're going to have to swim but I'll hold on to you, I promise. I'll keep you safe."

Vivi just shakes her head, a groaning noise coming from her lips as she looks at the water in terror. It's like whiplash, the way she switches from aggressor to victim.

"I can't leave," she whimpers. "What is everyone going to say when they realize what I've done?"

Morgana looks at her; the girl who has wreaked chaos and devastation on Avalon. Maybe not single-handedly, she can see that;. they've each had a part to play, some bigger than others. Not all the damage caused this summer can be healed, not even with time, effort or all the money in the world.

"It's time to find out," she says. And then she wades forward, pulling Vivi off the rock and dragging her through the water towards the cave entrance, battling against the tide.

The water is cold, too cold, and the current is strong. Morgana feels her feet lifting from the floor and wraps her arm round Vivi's body.

"Try to float!" she yells, as the water pushes them up towards the cave ceiling. She just needs to make it to the entrance and the rocks that provide sanctuary further up the cliff face, but the tide has other plans for them.

"We're going to die!" screeches Vivi, her limbs flailing in panic. She grabs at Morgana, pushing her under the water in her desperation and Morgana has to fight every instinct that is telling her to let go of the girl who is now threatening her life. She wants to scream at her to calm down, tell her that her hysteria is going to kill them both, but she can't waste any of her precious energy on words.

Her head surfaces and she gasps for breath before Vivi yanks at her, pulling her under again. They're not going to make it. The tide is too fast and Vivi's fear is too fierce. Morgana feels the water pressing in on her from all sides as she sees the image of Sibilla coming towards her. And for a split second, she contemplates giving up and letting herself sink to the bottom of the cave to rest, if only for a few moments.

Fight.

The voice comes from everywhere and nowhere.

Fight, girl. Like you've never fought before.

And then the water changes. Instead of pressing in on her, she feels it flowing around her, nourishing her, invigorating her arms and legs. She feels every single drop, cold against her skin, waking her up and reminding her of who she really is. Her kicks get wilder as she focuses on the water above her. She fights for her life.

It ends with her. That's what Celeste told her. It starts with Celeste but it ends with Morgana. It's up to her to finish this and she can't do that if she's lying in a watery grave. There are so many things that she wants to do, so many people who she must make things right with. Some of them have hurt her and she's hurt some of them.

Love. Hate. They're just words. And words matter – but they're empty without actions and deeds to back them up.

Another wave crashes into the cave, wrenching the two girls apart as it surges forward relentlessly. Morgana tips her head back as she breaks through the water, getting as much air into her lungs as she possibly can. They've managed to reach the entrance and the waves are pounding the cliffs with a ferocity that she hasn't seen before. The only way they can survive this is to somehow get on to the rocks beside the entrance but she's exhausted and Vivi is unlikely to be much help –

Vivi.

Turning her head, Morgana stares back into the cave. There is no sign of the other girl and a moan escapes her lips as another wave crashes into the cliff face.

"Morgana!" The cry doesn't come from the water. Morgana spins round, and there, perched on a ledge beside the entrance, is the person she most needs to see in the entire universe, summoned by her thoughts. She points frantically at the water behind Morgana, who turns just in time to see Vivi's hand disappearing beneath the surface.

She doesn't pause to think about it. Inhaling deeply, she sinks down, kicking hard in the direction that Vivi went under, willing the water to work with her and prevent another tragedy.

It's pitch black and freezing cold. Morgana forces herself to keep going, even though every bone in her body is screaming at her to turn back. There's no way that she can find Vivi in time and if she doesn't come up for air soon, then they're both going to be victims of themselves.

Then something is there, brushing against her fingers like seaweed. It's hair. Morgana reaches forward and grabs Vivi's head before kicking harder than she has ever kicked in her life, up towards the moonlight that lights their path. As she pulls them through the water, she sees a lightning flash ahead, followed by the deep rumbling roll of thunder. For a second she whirls in the water, scared that the cave is about to collapse on top of them, suddenly unsure of which way is up. And then a hand takes hers and she doesn't know now whether she's hallucinating or if Sibilla, pointing with an outstretched arm, really is pulling her in the right direction – but she follows her, up, up, up, trusting in something that she doesn't understand.

The first gulp of air is sweeter than anything she has ever tasted. Later, she will swear that it smelt of apples. But now, as she uses the last of her energy to yank Vivi towards the ledge where a soaking-wet Celeste is lying on her stomach, ready to pull them both up to safety, her brain is empty of anything other than the need to feel Celeste beside her.

"It's going to be OK," calls Celeste, as Morgana clutches the rock with one hand and keeps Vivi's head above water with the other, as she coughs and splutters. And then a bright spotlight swings on to them and strong arms lean down to scoop them into the rescue boat before helping Celeste clamber down from the ledge to join them.

The coastguard drapes blankets round the three girls and they sit huddled at the bottom of the boat as it turns and speeds back towards the beach. Celeste wraps her arms round Morgana, holding her safe, and Morgana closes her eyes briefly, allowing herself a minute to acknowledge that it's over. When she opens them, she sees that Vivi is staring at them both with what looks like terror.

"How did you find us?" Morgana asks Celeste, reluctantly pulling away from the warmth of the hug. "And how did the coastguard get here?"

Celeste reaches out and holds Morgana's hand, her eyes now the colour of the midnight sky. "I got your note and I came as fast as I could," she says. "When I got to the beach, I saw Art waiting for your dad to arrive – he told me that you'd run off after Vivi and nobody knew where you'd gone." She smiles softly at Morgana. "I knew where you'd be, so I told him to send help to the cave and I came to find you."

"But you're a forest witch," Morgana whispers, smiling back. "You don't *do* the sea."

"For you, I do." Celeste squeezes her fingers tightly and then whips her eyes back to Vivi. "And it's a good job that I did. This is why I didn't want you to go looking for the killer, Morgana. Her brand of chaos could have destroyed you."

Vivi clutches her blanket a little tighter, retreating beneath it as if it can keep her safe.

"I know." Morgana squeezes Celeste's fingers. "It's OK. She can't hurt us now."

At that Vivi lifts her head. "I was wrong about you," she whimpers, her gaze flickering between the two of them before resting on Morgana, fear still evident in her eyes. "I don't know what you did back there or what the hell you've tapped into, but I'm sorry, OK? I'd never have gone up against you if I'd known how powerful you are." Her eyes flit towards Celeste. "And you. I had no idea who you really are but I can see it now. I should have known."

Morgana frowns as the boat starts to slow. On the beach she can see Art and her father and, behind them, a whole crowd of kids from Avalon Academy, desperately trying to see what the latest drama is.

"What is she talking about?" She stares at Vivi, who is now shivering uncontrollably.

Beside her, Celeste pulls her in tighter but says nothing.

The flash of lightning. The deep roll of thunder. Sibilla. The deep sense of something bigger than her giving her strength.

Morgana doesn't know exactly what happened – but she does know that Vivi is right to be afraid.

And then the rescue team are reaching out to help them clamber from the boat and wade through the shallows to the waiting crowd.

"Are you OK?" Gordon races forward, gathering Morgana into his arms. "Art called me to say there had been a fire – but by the time I got here you were missing. What on earth happened?"

Morgana shakes her head, enjoying the unfamiliar comfort of being pressed against his woolly jumper. "I'm OK," she murmurs. "I'm OK." She's reassuring herself as much as her father.

"You scared me." Gordon finally releases her and Art takes his place, pulling her into a quick hug before standing back to glare at her. "You really scared me, Morgana."

Morgana looks over his shoulder to where Vivi is being checked over by one of the coastguards.

"It was me." The words and the tears push themselves out before she can think about it, as if the contact with Gordon and Art has released something deep inside her. And once they start, they become as relentless and unstoppable as the tide. "It was my fault that Alice ran away. I saw her leave. I should have stopped her but instead

I just watched her go because I hated the way she made me feel." She drags a deep breath into her lungs and stares at the sand, grief shuddering through her body. "I'm so sorry. Everything that's happened is all my fault. And now two people are dead."

"Morgana, what are you saying?"

"I'm saying that I made Alice leave."

"No." Gordon's voice is gentle. "Alice leaving was nothing to do with you." His hand rests on her shoulder. "You were a child, Morgana. Nobody has ever blamed you for her leaving. For her death."

Morgana's head whips up and she stares at Art, who nods at her.

"I know she's dead," he tells her. "I've always known. It just felt easier not to actually have anyone say it, you know?"

"But if I hadn't come to live at Pendragon Hall, she would never have left." Morgana shakes her head, trying to find the right words. She has to make them understand. She's carried the blame of what happened to Alice for years and a few kind words from Gordon isn't going to change that. "She was happy before I came."

Gordon's hand grips her arm slightly tighter. "Morgana. You need to stop this." He glances at Art, concern etched across his face. "Alice wasn't a happy woman. And that night wasn't the first time that she'd attempted to *leave*. It was just the first time she succeeded. Wherever she is now, it has nothing to do with you or how you felt about her."

He reaches out his other hand and pulls Art in, so the three of them are huddled together. "We're a family. And we need to start doing a better job of acting like one."

Morgana exhales, feeling the weight of her guilt start to crumble and drift off into the night air.

Gordon releases them both. "Now tell me about what's been happening here tonight."

"Vivi confessed everything." Morgana closes her eyes for a second, as the reality hits her. She didn't do this either. It wasn't her magick that caused all the chaos. "She killed Lance."

"What?" Gordon's face pales in the moonlight. And for the first time Morgana notices that there's no wind. She looks up at the sky and sees that there isn't a cloud in sight. Wherever the thunder and lightning came from earlier, it wasn't the sky. Perhaps it was another gift from Sibilla to help her find her way home. "Are you sure?"

Morgana nods, her gaze once again seeking out Vivi. "She told me herself." She puts her hand in her pocket, suddenly worried that the necklace might have fallen out when she was in the water but, miraculously, it is still there. "This belongs to her," she tells Gordon, handing it to him. "It was hanging in the tree where Lance died."

Gordon makes a noise of distress in his throat. "I'm going to go and make a call," he tells Art. "Make sure your sister is next to be checked out and don't leave her side." Then he strides off up the sand, his phone already in his hand as he searches for a signal.

Art runs his fingers through his hair. "I can't believe all of this – we were supposed to be honouring Lance's memory tonight."

Morgana heaves out a shuddering breath. "I guess finding out who killed him is one way to honour him."

"You're terrifying, do you know that?" Art glances at her. "Terrifying but all right."

"Morgana." Celeste appears in front of her. "Can I talk to you for a second?"

Morgana nods at Art. "Give us a minute."

Art looks from Celeste to Morgana and frowns. "I swear to god, if you run off again, then I'm going to—"

"I promise I won't go anywhere, OK?" Morgana smiles at him and shoos him away. He glares but retreats across the sand, out of earshot but making it painfully clear that he won't take his eyes off her.

"Morgana," starts Celeste. "Can we—"

"I'm so sorry," Morgana interrupts. "I never really believed it was you, you know?"

Celeste's eyes brim with tears. "I thought I'd lost you back there."

Morgana reaches out and their fingers link together. "I thought I'd lost you too."

Celeste pressed her forehead against Morgana's and it feels like hello and goodbye, all rolled into one glorious moment that Morgana wishes would never end but knows cannot last.

The kiss, when it comes, is as wild as the sea.

EPILOGUE

It's dark in the cave, the only light coming from the flickering candles that sit on the ledges. Morgana perches on the rock where Vivi sat all those weeks ago, and gazes out at the distant sea. The tide is low and there's no risk of it coming in here for hours yet, but she prefers to keep an eye on it. Just in case.

Her fingers trace the outline of a shape carved into the rock. She sees them everywhere now, Vivi's sigil. She's tried several times to translate it but can't make sense of what it might say. Not that it matters. It isn't for her to know. Vivi has gone now. There are rumours around town about where she's been sent, but Morgana tries not to listen.

And Vivi isn't the only person who has left Avalon.

Morgana sighs, remembering the day after all the

drama on the beach and Vivi's confession. Gordon had wanted her to stay at home and rest, but her feet took her to the forest and the Witch Tree. Part of her knew even before she got there what she would find, but it still hurt more than she could ever have imagined. The note was tucked into the hole in the trunk.

> My sweetest Morgana,
>   I wanted to stay. I wanted to stay so badly, but I can't and I think you know why. If you need me, I will return.
>   Wanting is not the same as needing.
>   I think I love you too.
>   Your Celeste

Celeste was never meant to stay in Avalon. If Morgana is honest with herself, she knew it from the moment that they met, from the first time Celeste told her about Silke and the Gretel Sisters. It was there in the way Celeste guarded Silke's tree – her tree – in the way she asked her sisters for advice and help. Morgana needed her and witch knows witch. Perhaps she was sent by Brigid. Maybe Morgana summoned Silke unknowingly. However it happened, she was here and she was real and she was love.

And now she has gone.

*

Some things are still the same. Pendragon Hall is still too big and too austere and too much like a museum, but there's a hint of warmth trickling in, especially in the evenings, when Gordon cooks their supper and she and Art hang out in the kitchen. They're talking more, although there are some topics that are still off-limits. Nobody mentions Vivi or Lance or Ginny, although Morgana has seen her around Avalon on a few occasions.

Art tells her that they should probably discuss what has happened as a family, so that they can move forward.

Morgana tells him that they need to figure out *being* a family before they can open that Pandora's box. They're working on that, though. All three of them.

Some things have gone back to the way they were four years ago before her reinvention. Maz, Lettie, Ro and Iris have reconnected and are stronger than ever, their dislike of Morgana only beaten by their hatred of Vivi. Morgana almost admires them for the way that they've taken a crisis and harnessed it to propel themselves into the top-most echelons of Avalon Academy.

Maz, the self-proclaimed new leader of the group, who still promotes herself by putting others down. Weakness is not acceptable or tolerated, in herself or anyone around her.

Then there's Lettie, whose striking looks have finally earned her the modelling jobs that she has always craved. Kindness is not a quality that is required in the world she intends to dominate, which is helpful, as, from the interactions that Morgana has witnessed, it is a characteristic that she does not possess.

Iris, the sugary-sweet princess whose words have a sting in the tail. She's kindness itself – unless someone does something that she doesn't like. Morgana is almost impressed by the way Iris maintains her good-girl image while being a complete and utter cow. Almost.

Ro has positioned herself at Maz's right hand and is prepared to do whatever it takes to stay in the group – no matter who might get hurt in the process. Morgana helped to make her this way; she acknowledges that.

They created monsters this summer. All of them.

The Sisters. Far from innocent but, as they didn't actually kill anyone, Avalon Academy is willing to accept them as the highest power. They strut through the corridors of Avalon Academy, scattering kids left, right and centre as they yield to nobody, bad-mouthing Morgana when they think she's out of earshot.

Not that she minds.

She's a shapeshifter, and shapeshifters can't stay in one form for long. She did four whole years of fitting in, being popular and desired and feared in equal measure. Now she's ready for change.

She's still angry – that hasn't diminished. Celeste helped calm the noise, but Celeste – or Silke – has returned to her own sisters. And for now Morgana isn't interested in squashing the rage that is always bubbling inside her. There's a ley line that runs under the beach, she knows that, and, as she sits on the rock, she can feel the power flowing beneath her. The air thrums with possibility and promise — and the tiniest hint of threat if a person knows where to look.

Not that anyone at school is brave enough to look at her. The rumours flow: a river of whispers and sideways stares and the occasional online comment — she lets them wash over her like the waves on a stormy night. She doesn't need them to tell her who or what she is because she already knows.

Art was correct — Morgana is terrifying.

He was wrong about her being *all right*, though.

She is not merely all right. She is absolutely everything.

Outside the cave, the waves crash on to the sand. Morgana sits and stares, wondering if Sibilla the sea witch will ever show herself again. She thinks about her mother, and Alice, and her beautiful Celeste, who she wants with all her heart but does not need. There will be others, she knows that. They will find her when the time is right. She won't be alone for ever and for now she can look after herself. She is enough.

Eventually, when she's done with thoughts, she slides down from the rock and makes her way out of the cave to meet the oncoming tide, casting off her clothes until she is dressed only in her bikini.

Morgana wrote something once in her Book of Shadows, when her world felt like it was falling apart. Eight words that were a desperate plea from a sad, confused twelve-year-old girl. And it may have taken years for her to get her answer, years for her desires to align with the universe and its plans for her. But she is here now and, as the birds caw above her, she can feel that the true magick has worked.

I just want to know who I am.

She is the wind hurling itself around the clifftops. She is the earth beneath her feet. She is the depths of the ocean and the roar of the flames that flicker and dance inside her. She tilts back her head to watch the ravens wheeling in the sky above her. They belong to her now.

Then she starts to run, feet splashing in the shallows until she's deep enough to dive beneath the waves. And even though the water is cold, she is not. Because she is Morgana Merrick and this fire will never go out.

Spell for Letting Go and Moving On

You will need:

1 pink candle, for healing

1 white candle, for strength

1 blue candle, for peace

A few sprigs of lavender

Some pine needles

A small piece of birch bark for a fresh start

Moonstone for inner strength

A charm bag

I. Light the candles and recite the following words:
<u>As the Earth rotates, I leave the past.</u>
<u>What is done is done, nothing will ever last.</u>
<u>I've done things right and I've done things wrong,</u>
<u>But now I move on – my heart is strong.</u>

II. Place the lavender, pine needles and birch in the charm bag, along with the moonstone. Hold each one in your hand first, imagining any bad memories, guilt or negativity to flow from you while you charge the items with your energy.

III. Safely extinguish the candles.

IV. Carry the bag with you, allowing it to remind you that the past is over.

V. Once you feel that the magick is done, return the herbs and thank the earth for its gifts. You may cleanse and recharge the moonstone, ready for when you next need it. Then move forward, safe in the knowledge that your past experiences have made you who you are. And never let yourself forget that who you are is <u>one fierce witch</u>...

ACKNOWLEDGEMENTS

Writing this book has been a complete joy and made possible by the help and support of a number of people. I would like to thank everyone at Scholastic, especially Julia Sanderson, Genevieve Herr and Sarah Dutton. Also my fabulous agent, Julia Churchill – I am so lucky to have you in my corner.

A huge thanks to Erick Dávila for creating the book cover of my dreams – your imagining of the characters is incredible, and I love it!

To my brilliant family – thank you for your ongoing patience and enthusiasm. You will forever be my first proof-readers and your thoughts and suggestions have made this book so much stronger. Thanks to Georgia, Zachary and Charlie for spending some of your summer holiday reading an early version. Thanks to Adam for indulging me in numerous conversations about plot (yep – this book actually has some...) and character development. Thanks to Reuben for reading the first eight pages – I appreciate it, kiddo.

Finally, thank you to my wonderful readers. I'm not sure if I have manifested a life where I get to write books for you to enjoy or if it's just pure luck, but regardless I am so very grateful to be able to send Morgana, Celeste, Art and the others out into the book-world. I love hearing from you so let me know what you think of *Wish You Dead* – you can find me on social media at @westcottwriter or @rebeccawestcottwriter.

Happy reading, witches...